ROCK SOLID

Beyond the music, what really matters.

D0767670

ROCK SOLID

Beyond the music, what really matters.

TONY JASPER

WORD PUBLISHING

Word (UK) Ltd
Milton Keynes, England

WORD BOOKS AUSTRALIA
Heathmont, Victoria, Australia
SUNDAY SCHOOL CENTRE WHOLESALE
Salt River, South Africa
ALBY COMMERCIAL ENTERPRISES PTE LTD
Scotts Road, Singapore
CHRISTIAN MARKETING LTD
Auckland, New Zealand
CROSS (HK) CO
Hong Kong
EUNSUNG CORP
Seoul, Korea
PRAISE INC
Quezon City, Philippines

ROCK SOLID

Copyright © 1986 Word (UK) Ltd

ISBN 0-85009-075-X

Typesetting by Suripace Ltd, Milton Keynes.
Reproduced, printed and bound in Great Britain for Word (UK) Ltd by Cox and Wyman Ltd, Reading.

Introduction

I've been involved in the popular music business for fifteen years and have loved some of its sounds and people for longer still. I've spun and talked about thousands of discs. I've spent hours, days and months talking with artists about their music and the results have appeared in many books, newspapers and magazines.

I also have a Christian commitment. That is the most important thing of all and this faith has made me reflect and ask questions that I might not have asked otherwise.

Over the years I've discussed life with people of many philosophies and I've met a few musicians who have been Christians. There were few until five or six years ago. Now their increase in numbers is fast.

This book talks about the lives and careers of these pop and rock stars, and more. It zeroes in on their faith, the whys and wherefores and the difference it makes to say 'I believe in Jesus'.

Much of the material has come from personal interviews, recent and not so recent; often material is from reading, digesting and appreciating what other writers have found. I thank them!

This book covers a wide range of ideas and people, but I hope you will find something to interest you and above all to raise questions about you and your own beliefs and lifestyle.

TONY JASPER

To

Paul, Hazel, Anita, Wesley and Laura Davis for their love and friendship.

Thanks to Di Mansour, Sybil Rang, Martin Wroe, Strait, New Christian Media, Contemporary Christian Music, Paul Davis and many others for their advice, writings and views that in-part provided valuable material for this book.

Contents

Contemporary Music

Cliff Richard

Was anything wrong with the Beatles? Cliff Richard answered that question. He described them as four of the richest young men in the world without any spiritual convictions.

'Show business can give you fame and money, but it can't give you something worth living for,' he said. 'Take the Beatles. After all the drugs and transcendental meditation, they still feel they lack something. What happens when they come out of it all? They are still in the backwoods.'

When Cliff said this some newspapers responded with a story on Cliff versus the Beatles. They misunderstood. Cliff was not concerned with the passing glitter but with permanent values. He spoke as he did because he had found a faith. Not one that came easily, but one which took years of argument, debate, discussion and reading to find.

He encountered religious questions within the Shadows, his backing group and stars in their own right. Licorice Locking was in their line-up for a time but left the Shadows in 1963 to become a preacher with the Jehovah's Witnesses sect. While Cliff and the Shadows toured the world they had a lot of time with little to do other than await the next television or film direction, sound-check and so forth. Pretty often Licorice reached for his Bible and explained how the sect saw things. Some of Cliff's family joined the Witnesses and so did Shads' member Hank

Marvin, but Cliff decided that this was not the true meaning of Christianity.

Christians were relieved when Cliff took advice, and counselling from mature believers like Bill Latham, David Winter and his old English teacher, Jay Norris. Cliff was involved in various activities run by an Anglican church in North London. He went to the Crusaders group and general Bible study and went sailing with the church's young people. For a while Cliff said a little more than he told the press in 1964. During this time he was still working things out and he told people that he was thinking about God. While he thought, the hits accumulated in the charts worldwide and he was well on the way to becoming the most successful solo hit record artist in British music history.

However the time came when he no longer needed to search and he wanted to share what he had found. He chose to make his declaration at a Billy Graham evangelistic rally in London. In front of 20,000 people he sang an old-fashioned gospel song, *It's No Secret*. He gave his reasons for believing in God and told why Jesus had assumed such an important place in his life. The general press thought it would end his pop career or, at the very least, that fans would think him soft.

Cliff commented, 'Anyone who thinks a Christian is soft can think again. It took me a long, long time, to pluck up enough courage to tell the world "I'm a Christian". But when I did I knew I had scored. Now I can make something out of my life. Don't think those people who smoke marijuana or swallow pills are being tough. That's not toughness. It's weakness.'

It was a pretty scary business for Cliff, for anything he might say could be misinterpreted. The press and media were waiting for slip-ups and for the generalised statements that could be misunderstood. He talks of sweat pouring off him as he moved forward to make his statement of personal faith.

The day after he gave his testimony he was front-page news. Some papers proclaimed the end of the show-bizz Cliff and they found distraught fans who could not reconcile themselves to the idea that his new faith might mean the end of his singing career. It became a popular topic of conversation. And of course there were suggestions that the Billy Graham appearance was a gimmick to gain him yet more press coverage.

At first Cliff gave plenty of reason to suppose he might quit the musiic world. He talked of wanting to teach religion. He was quoted saying 'I must get out of show business as soon as possible. But how do I do it?'

He gave interviews to this effect which, at the same time, witnessed to his new found faith. He mentioned that one of his reasons for initially getting involved with religion was a desire to make contact with his dead father. But he then found the Bible lent no support to spiritualism.

He talked of giving up £100,000 a year in show business for a £16-a-week teaching post once he had qualified, an event in itself likely to be fairly far off since he had few academic qualifications. Meanwhile, he used his show business, film and acting experience to star in a film funded by the Billy Graham Evangelistic Association. In the film he starred as a double-crossing, drug-peddling, bed-hopping materialist.

By October 1967 he had decided against a teaching career. This was a wise decision. It would have been a waste of his potential witness if his outreach was limited to a small localised area. After all, as a world-famous pop star he could tell numerous people of his belief in numerous ways. Cliff commented, 'I admit I was foolish in considering teaching now. I thought it was not possible to remain a Christian and stay in show business. I now know it is. I shall continue my religious studies but I shall not become a teacher until show business gives me up.

'I know a lot of people will knock me now and claim I've swallowed my principles for money. But I haven't changed. I'm still a Christian. Since making a film for Billy Graham I've realised I can be a really active Christian in show business. I never wanted to leave entertainment – it was just that I wanted to do something positive, too. The film has shown me how to do it.'

It was similar when he found himself confronted with the question of 'Why Cliff is not the Rev. Richard' some ten years later. He told Charles Catchpole, 'The thought of quitting hasn't entered my head... Certainly not. While I'm an entertainer I've got this marvellous platform, for my religion. I'd be undercutting my appeal if I gave it up. Who would come and see the Rev. Richard?

He denied that his Christianity and his clean living were at odds with the rock world.

'Sure, there are a lot of unpleasant things in this business, as there are in many walks of life. And there's a lot of good about showbiz. A lot of work is done for charity, for example, and there's hardly any racial prejudice.'

At the same time as he made these staements in 1967 his record *The Day I Met Marie,* one of his own all-time favourites from his long list of hits, was rising fast in the British singles chart.

By now he had been confirmed as a member of the Church of England. When he was seen lunching at the Athenaeum Club with Canon Frederic Hood, Canon Residentary and Chancellor of St. Paul's Cathedral, journalists speculated on the reasons for what was, in fact, a purely social occasion.

Such events triggered speculation that Cliff's public testimony of faith was motivated by a desire for increased publicity and consequent increased record sales. Time has surely proved such suggestions to be groundless and it would have been assumed that the long hours spent with a youth club in North London were also part of this publicity trip. It seems unlikely. He could have got far more attention if he had found a girl, become engaged and then followed this with another story announcing the engagement was off.

There are always easier ways to get publicity than through hard work but Cliff never sought them.

He told people in a matter-of-fact style that he could no longer hide his faith. 'I knew that if I wanted to grow as a Christian, I must go to church regularly, testify to my faith and set aside a fixed time every day for Bible reading and prayer.'

So his life-style began changing. He became closely involved with church activities. 'I get a lot of requests to do church work. I feel it is my duty to do it. If it really came to a choice, I would hinder my career before my faith.'

Cliff's open faith soon resulted in him being sought as a spokesman on all manner of subjects, even other star's lives. As well as the Beatles Cliff took Mick Jagger to task. The Rolling Stones lead singer was much given to speaking out on questions of morality and when he announced he was going to live with his girl friend, Marianne Faithfull, without being married to her the press naturally wondered what Cliff thought.

'As a Christian I wouldn't live with someone to whom I wasn't married. If you throw marriage out of the window what do you put in its place?'

Cliff also advocated a more responsible attitude to drugs by some pop singers and he reminded them of their influence.

'When pop stars spout that drugs are good and harmless

and are so blatant and cocky about it, they're being utterly selfish. No one in his right mind can say they don't give a damn what other people think without being totally heartless. I just don't understand how people can believe drugs are good, right or healthy. Anyone who takes drugs eventually realises it's a losing game.'

He said, 'You don't find Christians drugging around and sleeping around because we have a set of rules that keep us to a different style.

'I believe pop stars should accept that they do wield influence, and should use that influence responsibly.'

He kept popping up at all kinds of events and happenings, and, not surprisingly, often met the church hierarchy. A meeting with Dr Donald Coggan coincided with the publication of David Winter's excellent biography of Cliff, *New Singer, New Song* and Dr Coggan's *Prayers Of The New Testament*. Since Cliff was a star, David's book received enormous press coverage, reviewers being especially interested in reading why Cliff hadn't married Jackie Irving, who was later to marry Adam Faith.

There was a great deal more in David's biography than Cliff's romances. The main story the book set out to tell dealt with Cliff's gradual realization that he belonged with those who wanted to follow Jesus. He spoke at small and large events although it wasn't always possible to do so without the razzamatazz of the pop world.

Cliff could be no more like the average person in the street than a cow can masquerade as a pet terrier. He was what he was, a world star. For some people the sudden proximity of their favourite star – just a few feet away talking easily about his personal beliefs – was a little too much. Fortunately they generally fainted rather than screamed. The press followed him avidly as if waiting for a sudden denial or the acknowledgement of the publicity stunt of the century. At the same time this attention from the press meant they were constantly telling their readers of his deeply, held Christian convictions.

One major newspaper ran a headline 'Packing Them In' and in fairly large capitals exclaimed beneath 'PREACHER CLIFF RICHARD'S SALVATION SONGS NEARLY BRING THE CITY TO A HALT.'

The opening paragraph read:

'There are those who imagine that the religious beliefs of Mr Cliff Richard may dent his popularity. Let them study this extraordinary scene.

The setting is Kingsway Hall, home of the West London Mission (now at Hinde Street, London W1). The hour is lunch-time yesterday. Cliff is preaching the gospel, and the "flock" has gathered. Mini-skirted, maxi-coated office girls had rushed from their office. They brought sandwiches and apples to eat while they listened . . . Cliff talked and sang to his own guitar accompaniment. Somehow everyone was so absorbed that they lost track of time. In the end Lord Soper, superintendent of the mission, reluctantly had to call a halt.'

There was also publicity for charitable events and his support for various moral crusades of the time. Predictably all kinds of newspaper and magazine reporters queued for interviews.

'I want to be an active Christian. You can't be a teenage idol for ever but you can go on selling records. I'll sing, dance and do comedy sketches. I believe in being myself and not trying to be something I'm not.

'I'd like to be married. That is, I'd like to have a wife and children. But that's not a good enough reason to get married. If you're a Christian like I am, you need to feel a real spiritual affinity with someone.'

Of course the press loved the last remark. They had always looked for romance in his life but now there was a different angle. It was not merely a question of whether he would find the right girl but if he would find a Christian girl, an important difference.

When I wrote *Cliff* (with Pat Doncaster) and later *Silver Cliff* I had access to his diaries and I remain impressed still with the amount of routine Christian work he got through where somehow he did escape the national though not always the local press. There are more effective ways of furthering a world pop career than talking with an unknown church youth group or school in a small town. All the more so now time has passed and there seems no sign of his falling away. He continues to be a strong active Christian and very much involved in charitable activities.

At the time of his conversion and since there have been those who wish he might say or do things more in line with their thinking. Also there are those who criticise what he does but cannot say what they think he should do. There is a group that wishes that he would both leave the pop scene and witness to it! He has his share of hate mail, some even from professing believers who have either not met him or are ready to believe anything they hear.

The plain truth was that a pop star had become a Christian who still strives to share and live his faith. In the years since he has had to suffer all kinds of labels, perhaps the most irritating being 'Mr Goody Goody'. That has rankled with him and during Live Aid when he heard the same name being applied to Bob Geldof he remarked how glad he was to share the title.

In 1968 Hodders published *The Way I See It*, at the price of 3/6d! On the back sleeve he wrote:

'Since it got around that I was a Christian – especially since I stood up at that Billy Graham rally back in 1966 and said so openly – I've been deluged with people wanting my views on all sorts of things to do with religion. People write to me, stop me after shows and pin me in corners to find out what I think about God, Christ, the Bible, the Pope, Billy Graham, adultery, drugs, apartheid, Vietnam, the end of the world and just about every other subject.

In this book I've tried to answer most of the questions people ask me about all kinds of subjects.'

The book was written for people who bought records and read teenage magazines. Cliff told in enthusiastic terms the story of his conversion, his new found joy and peace and he was careful to relate his life as a pop singer to his faith especially answering the criticism of him remaining in a pop world that some of his critics saw as totally evil.

He mentioned how, during his run with the Shadows in Cinderella at the London Palladium, he was asked, 'What is your favourite thing at the moment?' Previously he might have mentioned cars, sailing, swimming or girls. Now he answered 'Sundays'. The remark was picked up by some newspapers who expressed surprise at this answer. Cliff talked of how on Sunday he could have a relaxed Sunday dinner, then go to Crusaders – the Bible class where he was an assistant leader. After tea with some friends he would attend the evening service at his church and afterwards go to the Youth Fellowship meeting in the church hall to enjoy guitar playing and some really good singing.

He commented 'To some people, that may sound like the biggest drag on record. In fact, I mean it when I said it was "my favourite thing". I can't believe anybody "living it up" in the West End could possibly get the satisfaction I do from an ordinary, quiet, routine Sunday *as a Christian*.' He proceeded to answer other criticisms people made of the Church and concluded: 'I think people raise these trivial things as excuses for staying away from church and won't listen when Christians try to answer them. The truth is, they don't know what they're missing!'

It was a point he would make continually – 'you don't know what you're missing' and it was a theme he carried into many publications where previously the idea of an article on any religion, let alone on Christian belief, would not have been considered.' Outside of angling, mountain climbing and crochet magazines he was everywhere!

On 23 May, 1970, he adorned the pages of *Mirabelle,* a girl's magazine rather given to the theme of falling in love. He was asked about the cult interest that had permeated youth thinking at the end of the 1960s and early 1970s. The particular cults the interviewer had in mind were not religious groups but rather youth cultural expressions such as 'skinheads, Hell's Angels and hippies.'

Cliff replied, 'Personally I don't mind the cults at all, the youngsters can dress how they please. What I do abhor is the violence – from anyone. I can't understand people who get violent just for kicks. But that's why there are still wars, because people enjoy violence.' He added 'Christianity isn't a set of negative rules – it tells you what you should do as well as what you shouldn't.'

In *Rave,* another girl's magazine of the time and an accurate reflection of contemporary teen culture he spoke on a more personal level. Dawn James asked him if he found it very hard being Cliff Richard, as opposed to Harry Webb, his real name.

'No, I don't work everything out as people sometimes think I do. I think pop has to be spontaneous.'

When asked what was the driving force that made him become Cliff Richard he replied, 'I wanted to sing, that is all, I never imagined all this' (gesturing to the film set where he was at the time).

Dawn commented, 'With the recent press on Cliff's religious beliefs, one might imagine him to be a serious, goody-goody type of person, far removed from the dashing hero we once knew. But not at all. There is a dash of mirth and mischief in his honest face, and a ready admittance of human failings from his lips. Cliff is strong, he dislikes what is bad and looks for what is good. And what is good isn't all praying in church and being a little angel, and taking it easy. Christianity as Cliff understands it, isn't an easy way out. It is a hard struggle to live up to a standard.'

'I fight evil,' he said, 'If I think rotten things I hate myself. I try to be fair to people. Sometimes it is hard.'

The examination of the pop star turned Christian was also conducted in the popular music press. The *New Musical Express* on 28 November 1970 headlined:

'I'm as human as the next person – critics still hurt deeply.'

He told Alan Smith 'I'm not a complicated person, and I don't think I should pretend to be anything else.' He said he had been upset by a recent feature where the journalist had described him as 'mechanically charming' – 'I'm not going to pretend it didn't hurt me, because it did. Deeply. But what really stung was the realisation that here was somebody knocking me for trying to be pleasant and friendly. It made me wonder just what kind of world we're living in. I mean, I know we live in a topsy turvy world, but when it gets that values are turned upside down – then it's getting ridiculous. What caused the reporter so much hate?'

He was asked by Alan what he did with his life when he's not involved with show business. 'Apart from working for Christianity, I don't know really. I like pottering about in gardens, that's for sure. I love going around sticking plants in.'

Cliff talked of how audiences are so important to him and then developed more on the general theme of communication.

'Communication between people is the greatest thing in the world, and this is why, as an artist, I've always welcomed the opportunity just to stand up in front of groups of people and answer their questions. It's an absolute ideal.

'I appear a lot like this at Christian meetings, and it's still a great pleasure for me because, simply, my Christian faith is stronger than ever. I can't see myself falling by the wayside as a Christian. You can't be left behind as a Christian, otherwise the Gospel doesn't make sense. It just isn't possible to be saved one day and unsaved the next.

'You know, I really spent a long time thinking about the whole thing before I became a Christian. It didn't happen overnight. I talked to Jewish people, I talked to Jehovah's Witnesses and people who didn't know what they believed. It wasn't until I met Christians that I was able to say "They have got what I want. They have got what I'm looking for." They just told me they knew God, and had a personal relationship with Him. And that was it.

'I think it's a typical thing that so many people in the pop business and elsewhere have been looking to the East, and towards mysticism, in recent times. They got through a long period of saying "There's no God", and then as soon as meditation became popular everybody latched on.

'But I believe that Christianity has the only positive answer. Buddhism for instance only offers a relationship with God after trillions of years. With Christianity, it happens as soon as you, personally, understand enough about God to invite Him into your life.

'Jesus was the only one to claim divinity. And that, in itself, was enough to stop me looking into the rest.

'I don't think it's presumptuous to say it . . . but still I believe I have found the truth.'

Record Mirror in its edition of 26 August 1972 ran a headline

CLIFF RICHARD – A SUPERSTAR AT 32
– and he doesn't even wear a dress!

further down the page in a box of its own could be found the words:

– 'amid the current eruption of camp, gay, kitsch, sadistic, violent, ambidextrous and squalid exhibitionist idols, Cliff Richard, a veteran pop star of some 15 years experience stands in almost solitary wholesomeness. Is that image of gleaming righteousness, of immaculate goodness a thorn in his side?'

The writer probed Cliff's basic attitudes and inner feelings perhaps more substantially than Dawn James had in *Rave*. Veronica Groocock asked Cliff about the moodiness and broodiness that seem to be the trend amongst recent idols. She cited Marc Bolan as an example. She also pursued the 'goody, goody' image that had been attributed to Cliff.

'I don't want to be termed as "baddie, baddie". Everyone seems to think you've got to be really nasty, one of the boys, to be acceptable. Rubbish!'

Veronica admitted quite openly, 'There's no doubt that the Cliff Richard of today is a very different person from the rock star of the late fifties and early sixties – and this change has chiefly evolved as a direct result of Cliff's Christian beliefs.'

Cliff explained his Christian convictions for *RM* readers.

'Basically being a Christian changes everything – the core of what you believe in life, so that you become less selfish. Christianity is a complete turnabout. If you are egotistical you attempt to become exactly the opposite, and you develop humility.'

He was asked what kind of life he lived before he was converted. 'Well, I was never really an out-and-out bounder. I mean, it was a laughing joke – the boys were always saying when are you going to retire? We'd come off stage after concerts and we'd talk. And I always used to think "We had a great time on stage, and that's it – caput! Suppose it all finishes tomorrow?" I really became very dissatistified.' On his current feelings he commented. 'You can write songs about depressed moods, troubles, but you try writing a really happy song – you can't. The motivation has to be intense. And I don't think one can be intensely happy. If one is, the feeling is not as powerful as being intensely sad. You are not motivated, and therefore it's really hard to write things.

'I don't suppose any Christian should be totally content because you become more aware of the frustration of not being able to help in Vietnam and with the Irish problems and everything. On that score there's always discontent, but generally speaking I wouldn't swap the last seven years of my life.'

One aspect of his life that Cliff discussed with *Record Mirror* attracted other press coverage. It concerned his role in the Arts Centre Group which at the time was based at a house in Essex. Cliff had bought the property and he saw it as a centre where Christians in all the art fields could meet. They could share their problems and worries, gain strength and encourage each other as well as enjoy valuable Bible study and prayer together.

At the time of *Record Mirror's* article the Arts Centre Group had just run a multi-media arts festival. Groups featured included the Settlers whose lead girl singer Cindy Kent was a Christian who attended Cliff's church. Her witness had been a great help to Cliff. One newspaper dubbed the ACG the 'Club Where We Met'. Their reporter asked, 'What do Cliff Richard, Roy Castle, Thora Hird, Derek Nimmo, Dana and the Queen's press officer, Ronald Allison, have in common?'

The answer was simple – they all belong to the ACG, termed a club where they could meet for a drink or a meal to chat about their favourite subject. Not the entertainment business. Not the tax system. Not even themselves. They talk about GOD. The Centre still thrives. It has moved home a few times and has been settled for some years in Short Street, London, in the area around Waterloo station.

Music papers carried the saga of Cliff the Christian into the mid-1970s. *Melody Maker* on 18 October 1975 proclaimed in their headline CLIFF'S ROCK OF AGES. 'While others have shown the wear of hard times, Richard looks fresher than ever. It's remarkable to think that he has never allowed time to catch up but always remains, if not a step ahead, at least in line with latest fashions.'

In 1977 Cliff's up-dated autobiography appeared, *Which One's Cliff?* and became a major seller in the paperback market. In part it provided an answer to the old question – 'What is it like to combine a passionate Christian faith with all the glamour and glitter of the showbiz circuit?' The introductory blurb stated, 'Once called the "bad boy of pop" (this was during his early pop days in the late 1950s) and "too sexy for television", Cliff Richard is today acclaimed the world over as a top entertainer – yet he still finds time to visit refugee camps in Bangladesh and missionary outposts in the Sudan.'

Indeed the latter brings up another astonishing facet of Cliff the Christian pop star. Cliff's charity workload is phenomenal. Few others in his field can compare. Through the years Cliff has performed countless concerts, not only in a small way for the Arts Centre Group but on a larger scale for the Christian relief charity Tear Fund. One particular visit overseas as part of his charity work took him to Bangladesh and it's always been seen by Cliff as one of the most devastating times of his life. When he came back he told the press 'I'll never be the same again' and commenting in his book he says, 'It's what I actually said when I returned and with a few years' hindsight, I believe I was right.' In the book Cliff explains why he became so involved with Tear Fund when as a young Christian, he wanted very much to be useful.

'It's business was to channel gifts from Christians in Britain to enable Christians in needy places around the world to get stuck into relief and development work. In most cases, that meant coming alongside missionaries involved maybe in preventive medical programmes or agricultural training ... the point was that it was aid given always in the context of an evangelical Christian witness – and that appealed.

'The concept of Christ being concerned about the needs of "whole" people was clear enough in Scripture but somehow it had never registered forcefully before.'

His work for Tear Fund began with a concert in London's Albert Hall, in 1968.

'David Winter devised the theme of "Help, Hope and Hallelujah" and it was the first time I appeared on a platform without a repertoire and a backing group of old faithfuls. No *Living Doll* or *Lucky Lips,* no Hank Marvin, Bruce Welch or familiar session musicians. In their place were numbers like *It Is No Secret* and *What A Friend We Have In Jesus,* and on stage with me were the Settlers folk group'.

There was much more and his book should be read for the complete story. But his work has continued unabated.

Among other books and booklets from Cliff two predominate. In *You and Me and Jesus* Cliff explores Scripture and in *Mine To Share* he explains how he sees the Christian faith and why he commends it.

How has the pop star Christian seen his Christian experience over the years and how has he viewed gospel music in general? He says his conversion instead of narrowing the world, enlarged and broadened it, enabling him to see his career in a new and more positive perspective. He has seen his career as part of God's ordained plan for his life.

'If I find a really good gospel song, I'll do it because it merits being sung ... not because its "Christian"... Personally I make sure what I sing is not anti-Jesus or anti-God; that it is glorifying to Him. That's the kind of freedom we need in Christian entertainers'.

He continued, 'I keep thinking that when Jesus was here, they told Him "You're a religious man. You should be in the temple, not there with prostitutes, sinners and tax collectors." They still say it today. "You're a Christian, you should only be singing gospel music." But Jesus has liberated me; he enslaved me to Him, which gives me total freedom to do everything in His strength. For a long time I was told I shouldn't be in the secular world of entertainment. That's not really a criticism, but Christians are beginning to realize that there is a world of entertainment and that all art forms are created by God ... I don't feel I've got to sing about Jesus every minute. It's simply that when I get the chance to do so ... I do.'

He talks of Christians needing to be ten steps ahead of the world and not, as is sometimes true, ten steps behind. And he certainly feels that they should be found where action is.

'We do live in the market place and there isn't anything worldly which we must actually keep away. We're supposed to get in and change it. How can the salt have any value unless it's actually sprinkled on the areas of need? How can anything change without more Christians who are willing to come in and stand up for what they believe within the art world? It isn't just in rock and roll but we need Christian opera singers, classical musicians, playwrights, actors and directors.

'I don't want to sound trite and pious. I sing a song called *Why Should The Devil Have All The Good Music* and it sums up what I feel about my involvement in rock and roll! If I and others like myself came out we'd leave it all to the Devil, because he'll take whatever we give him. God created everything, every form of music is His. We can either take it saying "this is God's and we're to glorify Him with it" or we leave it, and believe me the other chap will take it.'

Cliff said that all too often all rock and pop artists are regarded as no-gooders. 'From reviews of my concerts I'm still an enigma as far as some people are concerned. They don't understand me and I find that rather a thrill because I know that is what makes my concerts different and difficult for them to review. I don't fall into the category of those that spit and curse and ruin first first class aircraft seats, so they find it hard to believe I can actually do what I'm doing. They think there is only one way to be a rock and roll singer – to be involved in sex, drugs and all kinds of violence. But I'm saying that's not true and proving it.'

What enables him to continue? He says it's due to the support of countless people at all levels. In Christian terms he rests upon massive prayer support. 'There are four people in my church with whom I meet once a month if we can make it, and I just open up to them, letting them know how I am. They pray for me specifically too. When I have that kind of support I know I'm not alone when I am on tour.'

But it's not easy for a star to keep in touch with reality however matter-of-fact he might be, as indeed is the case with Cliff. Nor is it easy for him to fight off criticism in spite of trusting people will take his words and hear. Cliff finds some of his show-biz activities attract critics who do not like the emphasis upon personality in the music world or the glam and glitter. They certainly cannot see why he should be in shows where there are gyrating disco dancers. They call it flirting with the world.

In the meantime, Cliff continues with a multitude of activities – radio; TV interviews; student discussion groups; church appearances; films; the opening of Christian bookshops; involvement with the ACG and Tear Fund; the fund raising activities for charity; evangelistic crusades; books; and, of course, records.

Records, for instance, are the bread and butter of his life. Whatever may be his Christian activities he still has to find success in the music world. On a few occasions he has had the odd bad spell when things have seemed a little slow, but always he has come back fitter and better than before. Much of his opportunity for evangelism depends on the success of his records and concerts. When his records succeed the interview demands flood in bringing opportunities to share his faith. Doubtless he would continue to enjoy some attention if the pop hits ceased but the mass media would soon lose interest.

There's been no sign that his special 'religious' albums have excited the media. Certainly these albums have had some fine material, *Good News* and *Small Corners* have allowed him to tell the old, old story of faith with a spate of new and often highly rated songs.

At one time his gospel concerts were pretty simple affairs. He came and sat on a stool and sang, sometimes talked, all very informal and relaxed. These days the concerts are more elaborate, and only slightly less so than some pop dos. But he still goes to schools and colleges, evangelistic meeting and, along with religious manager Bill Latham, he will talk and answer questions and maybe sing a song. Some of his 1980s pop material has had a clear religious strain and there has been more introduction of gospel into general bookings. His album *Now You See Me,*

Now You Don't had some very strong material, and Word, a religious record company, issued a most successful compilation of general material he had recorded for EMI. In the atmosphere of a nightclub he makes his witness clearly by often singing unaccompanied a hymn such as *When I Survey The Wondrous Cross.*

But what might happen at a gospel concert? Take a concert in 1983 in Brussels. Garth Hewitt, a genial talented singer-songwriter and good friend of Cliff's sang through the first half. He has built up a vast repertoire of material, his lyrics are always relevant, the music strong and he has a natural performing air. He was fine to preface Cliff.

Cliff started with *Why Should The Devil Have All The Good Music.* After a word of greeting for the audience he sang *Where Do We Go From Here,* then with guitar *It's The Only Way Up.* He explains in haphazard ways his difficulties in speaking the native tongue. He sings *Song for Sarah,* next *You Need A Light.* Cliff talks some more. He announces the next song as something special. It turns out to be the first gospel song he ever wrote titled *Son Of God.* It's a ballad and he tells everyone that at first he wondered about his faith but not now. He talks of being helped by Christian friends. He sings *Lord I Love You* and talks of how much goodness has come his way. He says, 'I have God to thank and I have to be prepared that he can take it all away from me.'

We Don't Talk Anymore follows. He tells how his next song is in the British charts, *True Love Ways.* He proclaims 'Jesus is alive today' and does a series of songs, *Yes He Lives, Up In Canada, Be In My Heart, Whispering My Love. I Wish We'd All Been Ready* and *The Rock That Does Not Roll.* He moves to a hymn *How Great Thou Art* and asks for audience participation. They do. The bank, back-up singers and Cliff leave the stage. Only Cliff reappears. He stands there and sings *When I Survey The Wondrous Cross.*

People go home. Some have found it good entertainment while others have deepened already established Christian convictions. Some will decide to seek further.

The gospel concerts, apart from contributing to Tear Fund, have produced many converts over the years. At these concerts Cliff began using a new term to describe his music – Rockspell. He explained, 'I did so because it conjures up exactly what we as Christians want to say. I don't know how to do anything else, except rock and roll, it is all I have ever known and loved all my musical life, and to combine the Christian message with the music that you make turns it into Rockspell, but it is no different to any other kind of music. It is just that we are far more positive about our approach to life, and therefore our messages are more positive.'

During the 1980s Cliff has had a powerful semi-documentary series on his life with particular emphasis on his faith. Radio specials are numerous, all opportunities to tell the message some more and reach different groups of people. He has made several appearances on the BBC-TV series Rock Gospel, presented by Sheila Walsh whose story appears elsewhere in this book. And of course he has made a number of appearances at the British Greenbelt festival held annually at the end of August. In 1986 he starred in the musical *Time* at the Dominion Theatre, in London's West End.

Along the way there have been a few hiccups. It would be surprising if there had not. He has always regretted the controversy that blew up over his recording of *Honky Tonk Angel,* a single that was quickly withdrawn leaving Cliff to explain that he was not really aware that Honky Tonk angels are ladies of disrepute.

More recently anti-apartheid supporters launched an attack on him for his visits to South Africa, raising the issue during his guest appearance at a Billy Graham campaign meeting in Sheffield. The Bishop of Sheffield, the Rt. Rev. David Lunn led the delegation from the city's anti-apartheid movement and asked Cliff to sever his links with the country that had led to his blacklisting by the United Nations. Cliff pointed out that he had not done a commercial concert in South Africa for ten years. His previous engagements had been made on the basis there would be no segregation. Cliff said he would still go and said, 'I go for one reason and that is to do gospel concerts and raise money for black problems'.

The genuineness of his faith is still questioned although it's a long time since 1966! During 1985 a British music paper weekly made some unpleasant insinuations about his faith. For once, enough was enough, and the paper was taken to the courts for libel. They duly apologised and a sum of money was paid into a charity of Cliff's choice.

He was asked on BBC Radio One by DJ Simon Bates, 'You live your life by a set of Christian rules, and I would think that very hard?'

'Yes. I would say it is the hardest way of life that is known to man. There is nothing that is so demanding, there is nothing so specific, and nothing so positive. Christianity comes and makes positive demands. It says that Jesus is the only way to God.'

He was asked about Band Aid and he replied with reference to Bob Geldof, 'I don't know what Bob and others feel about spirituality; goodness is not exclusive to Christianity, only salvation is. Goodness is something of which most people are capable, and sometimes actually live out as best they can. When I saw that (Band Aid single) I thought, "Well Whoopee. Here is an industry giving that is renowned for taking." '

In the meantime he continues along his chosen path.

Nick Beggs

It's not a nickname most people would like but it suited Nick Beggs that his fans should affectionately call him 'fluffy chicken' on account of his hair style. His mop has even been described as a 'peroxide explosion with beads'.

Nick was the youngest member of Kajagoogoo, a new British band formed in the 1970s from the less successful band The Leighton Buzzards. He became lead singer when Limahl, the vocalist from the band's first and massive selling single, left to pursue a solo career. The title of the hit *Too Shy* certainly did not apply to Limahl and to his future success as a solo artist.

Nick's first lead vocal was with the 1983 release *Big Apple*. Since then Kajagoogoo have built a world-wide reputation despite several failures. Nick joined Stuart Neale, Steve Askew and Jez Strode. They were a group who had attracted the interest of record companies early. After a showcase gig at London's Embassy Club EMI got their contract. Their early musical philosophy was straightforward. Nick said, 'The band was started mainly because we wanted fulfilment in our home town. It was a suppressive environment without a lot of opportunity to do anything of stature.'

The group soon repaid the faith of EMI with massive and instant public reaction to a catchy single *Too Shy* that relied heavily on the repetition of an infectious title hook. After Limahl's departure the band was thrown into a little disarray but in the event it gave them a greater degree of self-assurance, enabling them to launch themselves as something more than a pop group with a much photographed lead singer. Kajagoogoo had aspirations to move towards being a group with a more diverse appeal.

Big Apple, the first single after *Too Shy,* had been inspired by the group's brief visit to New York. Not too much of a change of direction there but the change was certainly felt when *Lion's Mouth* was released in February, 1984. Kajagoogoo felt it clearly displayed what they were musically interested in and a single from their album, *Islands,* entitled *Turn Your Back On Me* told the story to the much wider audience than the 45. EMI felt the album was an ideal showcase for the many aspects of their songs and they explained that the lack of overt pop appeal brought their musical, lyrical and songwriting abilities further to the fore. Nick told music writers, 'I want to entertain people but I have to say something from the heart – we have to be truthful. For a long time we were writing songs based on the pop idea, and I think we all got bored with that.'

Nick's remarks attracted attention and the group explained they had had time to develop and explore musically. Time, they thought, plus the new album, would prove their worth. However, it was to have a mixed reception. *The Lion's Mouth* reached 25 in the singles chart and *Turn Back On me* only 47.

In 1985, Kajagoogoo headed towards another career crisis. Beggs, emerged as a personality in his own right, in part due to his overall geniality and friendliness.

Musically he can recall his first gig. He was 15 and the venue was a Baptist Church. The group, Jobert Lilead's Music, was heavy metal, a rather far cry from Kajagoogoo where the accent is on melody rather than a pounding bass and drums. He fell in musically with Frank Zappa and Joni Mitchell and for something a little more unexpected he has always named Weather Report and various jazz bands. Many were perhaps surprised when he remarked 'I don't listen to pop music very often but a good pop song is inspiring.' He stressed, 'I like people who can do things well; I want people to recognise that we can play reasonably well when they listen to our records.'

Nick Beggs was born December 15th, 1961. He was educated at the Leopold Primary School, Leighton Buzzard and then moved to the Linslade Secondary School, Barnfield. He took a further education course at the Cedars Upper College of Design, Luton. He was born with blue eyes and his hair probably brown. Few know for sure! He eventually reached a height of six feet one inch and tries to keep his weight below ten stone.

His parents separated when he was ten and he stayed with his mother and sister Jacqueline. He remembers his dad gave him a drum kit and when he was around fifteen he began learning acoustic guitar. Music was his life partly because school bored him and music was a pleasant diversion. 'Schoolwork was such a drag that when I left I decided that I would do something I enjoyed. Music was the best option. But when I eventually kissed my schooldays goodbye at the age of seventeen, it was to a foundation course in art and design.' Later, it stood him in good stead when he took responsibility for overseeing the artwork for the group's record sleeves.

His art school years were marred by tragedy at home. Sadly his mother had cancer and had, in fact, kept it quiet. She was already dying and he had the painful experience of watching her waste away. Her illness and death shook him to the core and stretched him almost beyond endurance. The news had come as a shock. She was the woman he loved so much and who had brought him up on her own. Nick was seventeen. As he says: 'Technically because of her age Jacqueline should have been taken into local authority care, and I had to prove to the authorities that I was responsible enough to be the head of the family. I was under quite a lot of stress.'

How did he cope? He told readers of his book *Nick's Mix* that dope provided one way out and increasingly became a prop. 'It was a means of floating away from the realities I had to face.' And the realities were hardly pleasant. He had to piece life together and even with help from family, friends and his girl friend, it was not easy.

He began to ask a great many religious questions. He could have thundered forth denunciations of the Christian God and he could have taken an extreme position of hostility. But he did not for, as he explains in his book, it became more a case of reviewing some of the ideas that he had turned over in his mind during his younger years. For a while he had dismissed religious faith as nonsense but gradually he came to believe otherwise. He talks of living a selfish, uncaring life as though there was something he must get out of his system and as if he had to realise the depths to which he could sink.

'I got involved in a lot of casual relationships, purely for my own pleasure. I used other people mercilessly and I caused a lot of pain. It didn't last very long, but while it was going on, I lost a lot of good friends, and others told me in no uncertain terms that they didn't like the way I was acting.

'Deep down inside I didn't like myself either. I realised quite soon that what I needed was forgiveness. I knew I couldn't expect it from the people I'd hurt, however much I said I was sorry. But I did need forgiveness from someone. I wanted to wipe the slate clean and start again.'

He found help in his search for faith and identity from one of his roadies, a keen Christian by the name of Ken. Ken explained to Nick some of the very basic things upon which a living faith rests. He talked about the meaning and significance of Jesus's life, especially why He died and how through his death God could be found responsive and longing to forgive.

'God's son, had come to the world in order to create the chance of forgiveness. Instead of us having to take the consequences, He (a perfect man in every way) took our sin upon Himself.'

Nick felt himself challenged and gradually knew he could only respond to allow this new power and life to take charge of him and lead him to become a new person, as if born again like a young child able to respond differently to life.

Many things had to change in his life. Dope was out. He believed it wrong to continue living with his girl friends. He realised that his faith would touch and change all aspects of his life. He had to sort out what time was the band's and what was his in which he could explore and study the meaning and implications of Bible teaching.

On the surface things progressed well musically but there were a number of things that had to be faced. Limahl's name was splashed across the British tabloid press for a supposed homosexual relationship with Paul Gambaccini. The band began attracting a hostile press and even some of the pop papers took a stand that made life difficult for new Christian Nick. *Melody Maker* had described the group in disapproving terms. They were seen 'looking like wooffers on the warpath' who 'generally made complete dicks of themselves'. This was in response to a 'pubescent shindig at London's Lyric Ballroom' for Capital Radio, London's main commercial radio station.

Some Christians asked what was a Christian either doing in such a band or mixed up with an outfit where the lead singer was subject to such newspaper gossip.

It was not an easy time. Nick was young in the faith to face the pressure and answer the questions in the context of his Christianity. Another challenge was that the band had to decide how they would prevent themselves being marketed as just another pop product to be put in a 'scream' setting.

He was fortunate in finding listening ears and friendship from the Arts Centre Group pop fraternity and particular support from Nigel Goodwin.

Many of these problems facing Nick were raised by *Strait* editor, Stewart Henderson, in the paper's twelfth issue. Nick had thought all the adverse publicity might have finished the band but fortunately he and the group survived the horrendous period attached to Limahl's departure and the rumours circulating about his personal life.

'We thought the fans wouldn't be there... we did a television show for the BBC the other week and it was very surprising because there was a whole crowd of completely different faces but of similar age to previous Kaja fans. They had big banners saying Kajagoogoo are still their No. 1.'

But what of the band, its future, and Nick's faith within an arena of record companies looking for hits and a band that might be looking for something possibly in conflict with Nick's new commitment. 'The question of compromise has been with me throughout my life, certainly as far as God is concerned. And because of that pattern of compromise I don't get as close to Him as I'd like to. As time goes on I hope I'll be able to make more sacrifices for Him through the supply of His grace.'

He denied the record company had ever steered him and the band towards a particular image or sound. When Stewart suggested EMI might have been saying 'C'mon fellers, Bay City Rollers time again', Nick thought they were saying that to Limahl but not to Kajagoogoo.

Stewart asked whether Nick saw the group's music as

having any lasting qualities comparable with say songs of the 1950s and 1960s which have inspired, for instance, Siouixsie and the Banshees, resembling Dear Prudence and Culture Club simulating Bobby Vee!

'I don't know. Everything I do now in music I do through faith. I feel that God needs to fill me up so that I'm doing what He wants.'

'What would you find incompatible with a music career in the record world and being a Christian?' asked Stewart. Nick said he would object to blatant sexual symbolism. He cited some German teen magazines which were questionable in their attitudes and had refused interviews with these journals. He felt he could not be interviewed and then find that the next page gave sex education to fourteen-year-olds and advertised contraceptives on the page after that. He also found it difficult to be put across as some kind of soft drug or product to feed into the fantasies of young girls.

He was aware that he must positively hold to his faith and that when asked to give his views on all kinds of things he could clearly state his Christian influences. His final remark to Stewart was, 'In God comes total sufficiency, although I've still got a lot to learn. A lot of people are looking up to me as if I've got profound things to say to them but I'm still learning.'

Nick's views led him to feel that some aspects of the 1980s music scene were less than savoury. He mentioned particularly that the occult seances of Iron Maiden were disturbing and Pink Floyd's Wall drama was frightening.

'I went to see the film. I think Roger Waters is surely bordering on paranoia. When I came out I gave thanks that I had God in my life. How awful it must be to have no hope, to see such blackness.'

He felt he had to provide a counterbalance to the gloom and despondency that pervaded the lyrics and life-style of the people he mentioned. 'I want to give people another option – I mean all this is relative, all insignificant when considered in terms of eternity.'

Nick considered for a time that he might join the Roman Catholic Church. His close association with Sal Solo ex-Classic Nouveaux, led him to a Catholic shrine where, like Sal, he felt the presence of God. It seemed part and parcel of an overall search for Christian understanding.

He remains true to his faith at the time of writing but his career is undergoing another upheaval. Kajagoogoo made little impression during the latter part of 1984 and none at all in 1985. To no one's surprise the group split and Beggs re-emerged in a new band called Kaja. In spite of considerable EMI publicity no success came their way.

There has been some suggestion that Nick's Christianity has contributed to both groups' lack of success but that seems unlikely. People like to place blame and certainly there are people in the pop world who are opposed to Christianity.

Rock People

U2

There is no quick and easy guide into Dublin band U2 although some basic facts are simple. U2 members attended Mount Temple School in Dublin where Larry Mullen pinned up a notice on a school board saying that he was forming a group and inviting potential members to apply.

Mount Temple was an unusual school in Ireland. It was the first 'comprehensive', it was mixed but most of all it was non-denominational.

Mullen received positive responses from Adam Clayton, Dave 'The Edge' Evans and Paul 'Bono' Hewson. U2 played their first concert at the school during the early part of 1978.

In November 1979 CBS (Eire only) released a three-track 45 with *Out of Control, Stories For Boys* and *Boy-Girl*. The same label, and again Eire only, launched *Another Day* coupled with *Twilight*. The first British release was Island's *11 O'Clock Tick Tock* in May 1980 with Martin Hannett producing and yes, there was a picture sleeve. U2 first came to London in 1979 and played a small number of gigs including one at a very popular venue of the time, Islington's Hope And Anchor in North London, near the Arsenal football club ground and the tourist mecca, Camden Passage. They also played the trendy but cramped Rock Garden in Covent Garden.

Not everyone knew who they were and at least some thought they were called V2, for that was how they were mistakenly billed in *Melody Maker*, the weekly pop journal. Then in another gig in Canning Town (better known for David Essex, West Ham and the Mayflower Settlement), at another 'favourite' music centre, The Bridge House, they noticed their name had become UR. It was a pity but they were confident that one day people would call them by the right name!

They came over several more times in 1979 and if *Melody Maker* got the name wrong at first, the magazine certainly made up for the error by subsequent praise. It was the same elsewhere, though *Melody Maker* was the most lavish. U2's first album, *Boy*, was released in November 1980 and enthusiastically received. It was recorded in Ireland. The four had mixed feelings about London. It seemed so worldly and they preferred the atmosphere of Dublin.

It is hard to assess the emotions, feelings and responses of the group, or the musical or spiritual commitments of the guys. None of this remains constant. An example is this – they released the superb album *War* in February 1983. The overall mood of this record was cautious. The group were hardly aware of the big world beyond Dublin but defended their perspective and their right to define their own style. They were criticised for following a safe format that centred around bass, drums and guitar but they were not interested in the latest technological trends and saw scope for development within the traditional framework. They preferred the human interaction this allowed.

Here is a group successfuly flying against progressive musical opinion and rising above the mundane. They are fresh, inventive and original.

Since *War*, U2 has broadened its experience. The guys have matured in many ways but are still characterised by an overall ease and a willingness to take risks, although not always successfully. In the music business faults are rarely acknowledged. When things go wrong a well-paid public relations person is used to edit the facts. But this is not the way for U2 and it means that the group can run foul of the establishment and be misunderstood in the religious world where, again, the members cannot be fitted into any neat pigeon-hole.

Barney Hoskyns, writing in Britain's musical paper, *New Musical Express*, seemed to understand this. In June 1985 he wrote of the integrity and honesty of U2, wondering whether some of the gestures and actions might be rather premeditated. But he was disarmed by the unswerving honesty reflected in Bono saying, 'Yes, what is it like? (to be a rock star). There must be people better qualified to answer that. I think I'm a part-time rock'n'roll star. We're probably the worst rock'n'roll stars ever. We've got all the wrong equipment.'

He continued, 'Part of it with U2 is the falling over and picking ourselves up off the ground, part of it is sitting up late at night in Philadelphia and saying something that will put a noose around my neck. There's a real love/hate thing with the group, and that's simply because we are experts at shooting ourselves in the foot.

'I met Elvis Costello a few months back and he said to me, "I'm ambivalent about U2. I love it and I hate it. You walk this tightrope that your contemporaries are afraid to walk. When you stay on it I bow my head, but you fall off it so many times," and there was no answer to that. We do fall off a lot. On stage I'll try for something, and it may or may not work, and that's the point. It might *work*.'

Few music critics or fans can accept that. They want every performance to sound like the record or else.

When it comes to their faith the same independence applies. U2 have expressed in their music, and often in interviews, strong passionate Christian elements. For example they differentiate between 'religious' and

'Christian', and the sectarian struggle in Ireland is the former, to their way of thinking. These sentiments are not expressed with religious fervour. U2 have never voiced straightforward sentiments about the Christian faith. They have not supported any particular mission or evangelist. Nor have they kept their faith a secret. Many people in the rock world, writers particularly, know the Christian commitment of the group. Such is the quality and power of their music that few would ridicule them on account of their faith.

The central theme of the album *October* is faith. Bono, who has always been the spokesman for the members' Christian convictions, has said, 'I believe in God very strongly and I don't believe that we just kind of exploded out of thin air. I can't believe it.

'I think it's that spiritual strength that's essential to the band. But people have got to find their own way. I'm not into standing up and saying, "Hey! You should be into God!" My own life is exhilarating through an experience I feel, and there's no point in talking about something which should be there in your life anyway. You don't have to preach about it... We get flak from all sides, really heavy letters from people saying... "How can you believe this and do that?" I'll talk about (those things) in the music.'

Author Dave Thomas emphasises that the opening track of *Gloria* puts these emotions into music. One critic has described it as the nearest rock music has ever come to producing a hymn, 'but not a hymn in the church sense, rather in the sense that it is uplifting, spiritual, a song of praise and glory, of power and love.'

Rejoice is the next to last track on the first side of this album. Bono says, 'I used the word Rejoice precisely because I know that people have a mental block against it. It's a powerful word. It's lovely to say. It's implying more than simply "Get up and dance, baby."' *Tomorrow* seems to warn of the Second Coming while other cuts like *Stranger In A Strange Land* talk of personal turmoil.

Bono talked with Terry Mattingly of the US journal *Contemporary Music* and explained his attitude toward speaking out.

'For a long time we haven't talked about the fact we're Christians because it's so easy for people to misunderstand.

'I don't believe in preaching at people. You know, I always include myself in the "we" . . . "We" have fallen. I include myself. *I Fall Down* is a song about my own failures. I'm not telling everybody I have found the answers.'

'I've spent most of life avoiding labels. I don't intend to adopt one now.' Of the music and its impact upon an audience he said, 'I like to think people feel it. They just don't want to allow themselves to feel it. I mean, everybody feels it. Everybody. So on *October* and *The Unforgettable Fire*, on *War* and the live set *Under A Blood Red Sky* there is joy and celebration but also the sad side of fallen humanity.

'When you look at the starvation, when you think one third of the population of this earth is starving, and crying out in hunger, I don't think you can sort of smile and say "I know. Well, we're the jolly human race. We're all very nice really." I mean we're not. People have got to see what is going on.'

The album *War* meets the last point. Bono says, 'War seemed the motif for 1982. Everywhere you looked, from the Falklands to the Middle East and South Africa, there was war. By calling the album *War*, we're giving people a slap in the face and at the same time getting away from the cosy image a lot of people have of U2.'

Edge added, 'It's a heavy title, it's blunt. It's not something that's safe . . . So it could backfire. It's the sort of subject matter that people can really take a dislike to.

But we wanted to fly a bit closer to the wind, so I think the title is appropriate.' *War* opens with *Sunday Bloody Sunday*. U2 bravely sang this at Live Aid, the sort of occasion that usually remains free from possibly contentious lyrics. While the song is well-known, relatively few of the world-wide audience of Live Aid would have been familiar with the lyrics.

For many, here was an Irish group with a fiery lead singer announcing a song that referred to the Irish question, although Bono always prefaces the song by stressing that it is not a rebel song. In fact it is simply a powerful indictment of all who would divide and who let hatred win over love.

Bono told the *NME*: 'We're not only interested in the physical aspects of war. The emotional effects are just as important. ... Instead of putting tanks and guns on the cover, we've put a child's face. War can also be a mental thing, an emotional thing between lovers. It doesn't have to be physical.'

He said how young people were becoming increasingly concerned with 'the bomb' and 'nuclear devastation' and he noticed the rise in CND membership. Bono said he wanted to confront people directly although he knew many would not appreciate this.

He was challenged, 'Considering the seriousness of some of its subject matter, *War* could have been a very grim and realistic L.P. But you also hold out a certain amount of hope.' Bono answered that hope was essential. 'Rock music can be a very powerful medium and if you offer something positive then it can be very uplifting. On the other hand, if you use your songs to convey bitterness and hate, a blackness seems to descend over everything... I don't like music unless it has a healing effect... Things might look very gloomy but there's always hope.'

He talked of the social pressures upon young people, with unemployment a major issue. He mentioned those who find life particularly hard to handle and who turn to hard drugs. In his area fifteen-year-olds are using heroin.

'I'm frightened, yes, but I'm not cynical or pessimistic about the future and a lot of that must come down to my beliefs. It's my belief in God that enables me to get up in the morning and face the world. I believe there is a reason and logic to everything.' The writer was quick to recognise Bono's Christian beliefs.

One line on *Sunday Bloody Sunday* simply says 'to claim the victory Jesus won on Sunday Bloody Sunday'. This provoked an American reader of a national religious music journal to protest, 'I question the Christian phrases in U2's album. According to tradition, Christ died during the weekend, and Sunday was not a bloody Sunday, but a glorious, victorious resurrection and completed the salvation planned by our Lord and Saviour Jesus Christ!'

However Bono was speaking about the overall victory Jesus has won for love, peace and righteousness over the forces of evil and despair. That victory is as real on a Sunday Bloody Sunday, such as the occasion of the sectarian disturbances in Ireland on the Sunday now given that name, as on any other occasion. In other words Jesus is Lord of all of life and his victory has application without boundaries.

The reader also referred to the song *40* from the *War* album and its use of the first three verses of Psalm 40. He asked the group for clarification on their Christian beliefs. He wondered whether they had the right cornerstone and if not 'it only takes me seconds to say goodbye. Please hurry on a reply. This is serious.' Bono will reply in his own good time.

When Bono speaks his words reflect an inner honesty.

He was once asked to speak at a youth meeting that would deal with unemployment. 'I could have said I'm one with them . . . but I realised I wasn't unemployed. I realised that I didn't want to speak at a committee meeting about rape, without someone raped being with me. I didn't want to speak about unemployment without someone unemployed with me. I realised there was another language, committee-speak, and I didn't understand it nor speak the language.'

For the album *The Unforgettable Fire* they brought in rock legendary figure Eno, once of Roxy and later an independent artist and producer of many imaginative and unusual works. Initially he turned them down but they persisted. Finally he assented, subsequently changing his opinion of the group and becoming sympathetic towards their views and objectives.

Bono attributes their eventual closeness to the emotion of U2 with its spiritual roots and Eno's love of the gospel music that had been his favourite listening for several years.

'. . . the sense of our abandonment in our music . . . people talk about the spirituality of U2 and I realised that though we weren't rooted in black music, there was something in the spirit that was similar.'

Bono's words about the single *Pride (In The Name Of Love)* are arresting. 'I originally wrote *Pride* about Ronald Reagan and the ambivalent attitude in America. I originally wrote meaning the sort of pride that won't back down, that wants to build nuclear arsenals. But that didn't work. I remember a wise old man said to me, "don't try and fight darkness with light, just make the light shine brighter." I was giving Reagan too much importance. Then I thought of Martin Luther King, there's the man. We build the positive rather fighting with the finger.' *MLK* was inspired by the late clergyman and civil rights campaigner. It is the album's closing track.

'Keeping The Faith' was the headline *Rolling Stone,* the leading US rock journal, threw across the top of their page in March 1985. The bold intro read, 'POP MAY BE KING, BUT U2 HAS ATTRACTED A FANATICAL FOLLOWING BY PLAYING THUNDEROUS ROCK & ROLL AND BY ADDRESSING SUCH TOPICS AS GOD AND POLITICS.'

Rolling Stone writer Christopher Connolly assessed the band's appeal. He dismissed the sexual aspect and suggested their strength lay in something deeper. 'Like most rock'n'roll bands, U2 articulates, at top volume the alienation that young people can feel from their country, their hometown, their family, their sexuality. Like some of the best rock'n'roll bands, U2 also shows how that alienation might be overcome. But unlike anyone else in rock'n'roll, U2 also addresses the most ignored – and most volatile – area of enquiry; alienation from religion. Sadomasochism is not taboo in rock'n'roll. Spirituality is.'

Indeed, when religion in America is often synonymous with political conservatism and with electronic evangelism, U2 proclaiming Christianity at top volume and suggesting that a person who loves rock'n'roll can find peace with God as well, makes a powerful statement.

Onstage and offstage this band rejects the yuppie maxim 'if it feels good go for it'. They do not ask how might we live our lives, what can we get away with, but how ought we to live our lives.

In this way the band speaks powerfully where the Christian voice usually only gets a cursory hearing in the occasional religious song from an uncommitted rock artist. The group speaks and witnesses in a manner that seems different from many emanating from inner strength and conviction. The witness comes through shining integrity. Some contradictions are apparent as the band continue to think their faith through very openly. Bono once said, 'There's a lot of plain old people out there (referring to the world), except I don't consider anyone to be plain. I think a lot of the vanity that is rock and roll at the moment is just people are afraid to look at themselves in the mirror. They're afraid of what they might see and so they just kind of cover up.'

For anyone who has heard their albums or seen U2 live in concert there is an air of celebration that overrides all else.

A letter in Britain's *NME* said 'Last night I saw them at The Longest Day (Milton Keynes Bowl day rock event). That one man can hold 50,000 people in his grasp for one-and-a-half hours is truly amazing to me. Bono's words "You are the nicest human beings in the whole world," would sound pathetic and unbelievable from any other rock star, but from him the sincerity shines through and you know he is genuine. The fact that it had poured down with rain all day was not enough to dampen spirits even slightly. U2 give you something to think about. You come away with a feeling that life could never be better. They do not hide the problems of this world, they help you to understand them and help make the world a better place.

'U2 bring people together. Everyone feels united as one, Long after leaving the concert the line from *40, How Long Must We Sing This Song,* still rings from the head. They are a voice for the youth and I want to thank them for this.'

There were elements of this in their appearance at Wembley in July 1985. But in their twenty minute set at Live Aid there was 'so much power, so much grace under pressure' that the artists seemed to reach right into the audience. With the final moving version of *Gloria,* a warm hand to the heart, clenched tight and a reassuring 'it will be alright', U2 were gone and Live Aid continued. During 1986 U2 made themselves available to Amnesty International.

After The Fire

'Look,' said the publicist, 'I've got somebody just up your street. You're a Christian aren't you? This band is into that kind of stuff. They're called After The Fire. How about a chat with them?'

I agreed reluctantly, the response of a journalist who had heard too many Christian bands who could neither play nor sing but wanted to say something without giving the musical goods. Some expected me to praise anyway so they could get some interest and give their message.

I met ATF in a tiny office at the top of some winding stairs in a building that seemed to be the home of women of ill repute. There was a mug of coffee that tasted of bad water but there was heating and the publicity people were friendly.

It's not all glamour. The band stood around and were natural and unaffected. They loved rock music and were determined to be good. My heart warmed, partly because I knew I could write about them anywhere and anyplace, and especially because they were obviously Christians with a strong testimony relevant to the culture of pubs, clubs, halls and recording studios. They wanted a record contract and the world beyond the stage of the church hall.

Another time we met at the Television Centre in a dressing room off a long corridor. They were recording a spot that would be broadcast the following week if their record *Der Kommisar* made the top 40. The dressing room was far from luxurious, it was bare and rather cold but roomy and with hot water. All quite usual, but then, less usual, we stood to pray. However, ATF's record did not repeat its high US placing in Britain. It stopped at 47, a sad failure that undoubtedly contributed to the group's eventual split.

ATF had begun in 1972, and was the brainchild of Peter Banks. He took a band around the South-East area of Britain for twelve months or so and then called a halt. After he met an engaging character called Andy Piercey who played electric guitar with gusto, ATF gigged again as a four-piece. There were a few line-up changes but along the way they were building up a following. By the end of 1976 ATF were finding things good. There was a demand for their services and they decided to turn professional.

A colourful character called Ivor Twidell brought some powerhouse drumming into play and the line-up was settled. They planned the first album but no record company came up with an attractive offer. Undaunted the group and friends, full of faith in their own talent and prospects, forked out the cash, recorded an album and formed their own record company to release it. Tracks were aired on Radio One and, having put down on disc numbers they had played for some time the band felt they could move to some new material.

More changes in the group's line-up occurred in the next few years. At one time they were down to a three-piece before guitarist John Russell arrived early August 1978. This was the year they signed with the worldwide company CBS (Columbia in the USA) and it was vindication of all the faith they had in themselves.

They had the musical goods; musicians, songs and a good act that had been honed through playing the rough and ready clubs with their discerning audiences who knew a good group, and would most certainly reject the bad!

ATF had done it their way and they believed it was God's way – that He wanted people out there in rock land with values, ideals and dreams. But they didn't imagine it would be easy and it wasn't.

There were a few shocks in store which could not have been predicted. But initially things seemed good. They were sent into the studios with producer Rupert Hine. He had been around quite a time and had a good reputation arising from his association with Quantum Jump and Cafe Jacques. It was 1979 and CBS issued a single title *One Rule For You*. It was attractive with a good title line and an infectious opening. It attracted DJ's and it had possibilities. For a while it seemed the group might have a fair-sized hit as it moved up the British listings. It reached 40 and stayed six weeks in the charts – another of those singles that on another occasion might, for no apparent reason, have gone much, much higher.

Some Christians complained that they couldn't see where the message was. Others recognised and accepted the band's subtle statements.

One Rule For You was culled from the group's first album, *Laser Love*. The title cut was to prove another chart single, though low-placed in the sixties. The album itself made chart inroads into the lower fifties. *80F* was the second album to chart, almost exactly a year later in November 1980.

Between the release of the two records, Ivor Twidell suffered a heart attack on stage and had to retire from the band. Fortunately, a few years later he was able to return to the music scene independently. Meanwhile Peter King, ex-Flys, took the drum seat. The first single with Pete was *Love Will Always Make Your Cry,* a few months before the release of *80F*. The group comprised Pete Banks (otherwise known as Memory Banks), Peter King, Andy Piercey and John Russell. It was a good line-up and had good chances of success. There seemed to be a constant flow of new opportunities and possibilities, and the provision of good album material kept expectations high. Moreover, ATF had established a fast-growing following and they were one of the better 'live' outfits on the road. The release of *80F,* their second album, was arranged to coincide with an extensive tour taking in some forty dates and climaxing with a sell-out at the 'The Rainbow' in Finsbury Park. The group acquired new management, Harvey Goldsmith and Pete Brown, a powerful duo that suggested there was now real drive toward first division rock status.

The group had a producer by the name of Mack who was riding high after producing top acts such as Queen and ELO. They felt he had found new dimensions to their music and given them even greater prospects of conquering the rock world. Hopes were high during the release and play-in of *80F.* The group talked of good record company relationships and they defended their new management deal. Material was mostly up-tempo, songs had some vibrancy. John Russell said, 'Things are going well, the tour was great and the record is a good one.' Andy summarised his position. 'I'm a Christian who is a musician and if that causes problems for people then that's their problem. I have to be aware of my responsibilities, however. Whether I like it or not kids look up to After The Fire. I don't see myself as a musician using music to evangelise.'

Talking of the band over the years and of his own attitudes, Andy said, 'I came into the band when we really felt it was something we should be doing; something God wanted us to do. We just took it one step at a time, and allowed ourselves to develop in the direction we were being taken.'

There were hassles with the record company over the next year and the album *Batteries Not Included* charted for barely two weeks. *Der Kommissar* seemed promising but somehow it did not live up to that promise. Everything seemed gradually to slip away. However, in the States a disco-remixed *Dancing In The Shadows* went into the top five following the success of *Der Kommissar*. The States acclaimed the band on a tour with Van Halen that began as a four week slot and became a fourteen week stay. Andy commented, 'As everyone knows, a Van Halen audience is there to see one thing – Van Halen – and quite frankly, we didn't know what to expect. So I can honestly say that we were overwhelmed when the lads asked us to stay on and finish the tour! While we all play rock and roll we're not really that compatible with Van Halen. I'd like to think that our music appeals to the mental as well as the physical needs of our fans. So the prospect of facing that crowd made us work much harder, and it payed off. We won them over.' As *Der Kommissar* soared in the US charts so *Dancing In The Shadows* was poised to take over. The future seemed so bright but its promise was not fulfilled.

Some time later I was at a packed meeting in London's Art Centre in Short Street. Andy and the others were there and I asked them about the sad decision that, even with high-riding US success, ATF would cease to function. Andy would continue the name, may mix some more tracks for the US market and steer a new course. The others would develop their own musical ideas. They told me about the problems and pressures; record company demands for hits, monetary difficulties and endless nights on the road. They had to watch potential hits being squandered for no apparent reason, and they shared the strain upon their Christian commitment during the ups and downs. Within the group, there was disappointment and reluctance that ATF should break up just when they had succeeded in America. But ATF had called it a day and a strong Christian influence was lost to the music scene.

In everyone's mind that evening were the thoughts of what might have been.

I know from my own correspondence that many young Christians felt elated by the band's success and overall ambition to establish good things in the rock world. There were also many who did not share their faith but respected them for having one. Faith endures, careers do not.

Bob Dylan

Dylan told author Anthony Scaduto, 'I like your book. That's the weird thing about it.'

Scaduto's book, published in 1983, was extremely good and he was one of the first writers to observe Dylan as a Christian. The only other writer mentioning this had been religious journalist, Michael Jacob.

When people wrote of Dylan they either penned superlatives or saw no further than the recording artist. Dylan was variously described as a 'great literary figure', 'cultural vanguard for dispossessed youth of the 1960s', 'a murky revolutionary figure', 'protestor', 'prophet of doom', and a mover from 'hobo camp' to 'high camp'.

Scaduto went beyond the surface. He recognised and related the inner conflicts that Dylan's outward behaviour reflected. Scaduto took the reader through the harrowing moments that came Dylan's way after March 1966, after the album *Blonde On Blonde* was released.

One graphic story tells of the girl who broke through police lines with a huge pair of shears and snipped off some of his hair. The incident plagued Dylan. He wasn't worried about the few strands of hair. It was what might have happened. The girl could have killed him. Friends said Dylan began to look like death and Scaduto tells of American folk artist Phil Och's comment, 'Dylan is LSD on stage, Dylan is LSD set to music... I don't know if Dylan can get on stage a year from now. I don't think so. I mean the phenomenon of Dylan will be so much that it will be dangerous. One year from now I think it will be very dangerous. One year from now I think it will be very dangerous to Dylan's life to get on stage. Dylan has become part of so many people's psyches and there are so many screwed up people in America. Death is such a part of the American scene right now . . . I think he's going to have to quit.'

Scaduto called his next chapter 'The Drifter's Escape'. He pointed out the Zen influence that permeated the songs on *Blonde On Blonde*. He observed the endless strains on Dylan's life – pressures of touring and being worshipped as a public deity together with the demands of recording. All these hindered Dylan's spiritual search.

Then came Dylan's motorcycle accident when he was riding his Triumph 500. It was serious and he was out of action for some time. He remained hidden for nine months and while he was incapacitated CBS-Columbia issued another *Bob Dylan's Greatest Hits* to tide things over. Dylan had time to think.

His next album came out in 1968 and if the Beatles, Stones and others had progressed into the electronic age of music then Dylan had gone backwards. As Scaduto put it, 'The electricity was muted, and his melodies had changed. They were simple folk melodies, only lightly emphasised by the tranquil backbeat, low-volume rhythm section – drums, bass, an occasional piano. And his voice was for the most part flowing more naturally than at any time before.'

The album was *John Wesley Harding*. It was Dylan's version of the bible. It was not just Jewish Bob travelling through the Old Testament. Christ and the New Testament were also under examination and his reflections were powerful, moving and convincing. *Nashville Skyline* didn't have the religious intensity of *John Wesley Harding* but its release fifteen months later in April 1969 reflected the change that had come into Dylan's life; he had a greater ease, a calmer, more meditative spirit. Between *Nashville Skyline* and *New Morning* was *Self Portrait,* described by some music writers as the ultimate low from which he would never recover. Some writers even called for a boycott of his music. The outstanding rock writer Ralph Gleason said quite clearly, 'We cannot make an artist do anything. Nor can we tell him what to do. But we have, I think, a debt to him and a contract exists between us. And that is simply never to accept anything less than his best.'

New Morning closely followed the release of *Self Portrait* and such was its intensity and high standard that Ralph Gleason exclaimed 'We've got Dylan back again.'

The album had one supreme and magnificent religious song, *Father Of Night,* that stands out as one of the greatest spiritual expressions in contemporary music.

This reflective period of his life from 1967-1971 was later recognised as significant when the rumours circulated and the whispers grew that Dylan's religious search had led him to Christianity. The Old Testament student, the Dylan who had gone to the Wailing Wall in Jerusalem and consulted many Jewish teachers and who had flirted for a while with Zen had seen the Old Testament scriptures foretelling Jesus. He accepted Jesus as the true Messiah, God's son, the final revelation until His second coming.

Indeed, from the time of the mid-1970s *Rolling Thunder Revue* (when Dylan swept through America playing surprise gigs with famous names in tow) and the film *Renaldo and Clara* that followed, he was persistently asking 'what will you do when Jesus comes?' It was a central and ever present theme in the albums that followed his conversion, beginning with the L.P. *Slow Train Coming.*

The music press carried news of his conversion with some hesitation initially but soon broke into an aggressive onslaught on his new-found faith. All observed that he was as much the object of speculation, myth and controversy as he had been at any other time of his life. In rock history he might well be seen as *the* figure of the 60s and his impact continued through subsequent decades to a varying degree.

His story attracted the general press as much as the music press. Headlines always seemed to have hints of jest, fun or sarcasm. The British music weekly *New Musical Express* had some of the best. Among their offerings came 'Heaven Can't Wait', 'Religion Today, Bondage Tomorrow', and 'With God On His Side'. 'Hail The Modern Day Profits' headed an article about Dylan and Little Richard that ended with the late Richard Penniman reported as saying 'I don't get expenses, I just do it for the Lord'. So the list can continue. Among the *NME* offerings was some pretty incisive writing, notably Michael Goldberg's review of Dylan on stage at San Francisco (17th November 1979) and Charles Shaar Murray's copy (during August 1979).

Many writers were obsessed with Dylan's appearance – perhaps they imagined he would assume an angelic mantle now he was a Christian, have his hair cut and make some attempt to look sincerely religious. Certainly there have been few people who have proclaimed Jesus before thousands looking so wonderfully malevolent with a 'great shaggy mane of hair topping a dusty white face, eyes hidden by shades and body clad in a sinister leather jacket.' Goldberg noticed his face was puffy and white as if he hadn't seen sunlight in weeks. Dylan's growth of beard suggested he hadn't shaved for several days and it seemed as though he had slept in his rumpled baggy black pants, white T-shirt and black leather jacket.

There was some more intelligent speculation beyond the sensational in the general daily and weekend press. This continued for several years, especially when he toured.

Mick Brown reported from Paris for Britain's *Guardian* when Dylan landed in the capital toward the end of June 1981. He arrived and departed in a helicopter.

Brown said he was not too surprised at Dylan's Christian conversion. He saw it against the background of the Christian revivalism that was sweeping America and thought that perhaps Dylan was being as true to the mood of the times and to himself as he had been in the sixties when he sang *Blowin' In The Wind*. Brown was not doubting Dylan's sincerity and added that the artist's recorded work since his conversion had shown some of his strongest musical performances. The albums he had in mind were *Slow Train Coming* and *Saved*. He recalled how folk fans called Dylan a Judas when he suddenly switched from acoustic to electric guitar at the Royal Albert Hall in 1966 and thought the times had stopped in 1981 with Dylan being accused of deserting his rock fans because he now had gospel singers behind him.

Certainly Bob's own attitude to his work and fans did cause alienation and as I have said in another book, *Jesus And The Christian In A Pop Culture* (Robert Royce 1984) he might have furthered his message if he had been willing to change his style less abruptly. He could have sung old favourites and explained that he no longer felt 'like a rolling stone' but he would sing the song as an expression of lostness and follow with another of certainty that had come from his new and living encounter with Jesus. But perhaps it's never been Dylan's style to worry overtly over his actions at the time though there have been later reflections which have suggested that he is not obstinate and pig-headed.

Dylan rarely gives interviews and so he created no opportunity to make his views clear or end speculation and gossip.

The religious press noted his conversion and hoped

readers would know who Dylan was. Those who had not heard of him could not realise the implications behind his decision. For those who had heard of him and who were committed to Christianity, Dylan's reputation represented the worst sort of worldliness.

The secular press also showed considerable interest in knowing exactly to what he had committed himself, but their comments were often purely speculative. Later more reliable reporting was forthcoming.

Contemporary Christian Music in the US covered his autumn tour of 1979, the first since his conversion. Legendary promotor Bill Graham was quoted as saying, 'These people paid their money to hear Bob Dylan sing the songs he is known for – they didn't pay to get preached at.' One of San Francisco's main papers *The Examiner* exclaimed 'Born Again Dylan Bombs' and the *Chronicle* shouted in its headline 'Bob Dylan's God-Awful Gospel'.

John Styll covered the tour for *Contemporary Christian Music* and remarked the 'man carried on, disregarding these comments, and told his audience in San Francisco "We are here tonight by the grace of God. That's the only power. That's what I believe." At the Civic Theatre, Santa Monica he said, "I don't know what God you believe in, but I believe in the one who raises from the dead."'

The Christian press, like the rock world's, would continue to reflect on Dylan's conversion as the albums appeared and the concert schedules were fulfilled. In August 1980, under large lettering, *CCM* headlined BOB DYLAN: SAVED. The double page spread – apart from two pictures – had page headlines that read 'The Saving Grace Of God' and 'A Sovereign Act of God'. The former developed a general theory that Bob's conversion seen in frequent scriptural reference and a striving for moral righteousness had its roots way back in 1962. Seay's article 'A Sovereign Act of God' was a study of Dylan within a more general framework of how can Christian artists be used in the service of the Kingdom asking what role can they play in bringing people to repentance and salvation? The writer observed that Bob's life and music had become infused with new and potent life.

Beyond the speculation and general observations, a number of facts relating to Dylan's faith came from interviews with people who had worked with or ministered to the artist. He had been baptised at the home of Bill Dwyer, pastor of the well-known Vineyard Fellowship on the US West Coast. He had attended a three-and-a-half-month Bible study course where the emphasis was on Jesus' life, the Sermon on the Mount, basic concepts in and demands for discipleship and growth, and the meaning of a decision for Christ.

Dylan gave a series of gospel concerts, donating proceeds of four Los Angeles performances to World Vision's relief work in Cambodia. He continued his Bible studies and maintained Christian fellowship. He sought counsel from mature Christians as he faced the clash between his faith and the secular record world, and his need to determine his involvement beyond the boundaries of gospel music.

The albums he released after his conversion were subject to considerable scrutiny. It was rare to find anyone who thought them unprofessional or lacking in merit but opinion of their content varied widely. *Slow Train Coming* was dominated by powerful, majestic numbers that relied on a gradual growth of intense feeling. The lyrics had some of the fire once associated with old-time preachers; the need to respond was set against the gathering storms precipitating the world's end. Vengeance and damnation permeated his thoughts with punishment never far away for the Judgement Day shall come.

Had he ever sung better? *NME's* Charles Shaar Murray

thought not. Others, more in sympathy with his message, thought people only found his words offensive because they did not want to hear songs about a cross of blood and pain; man damaged and warped by sin; and people living their lives in contrast to the strong, selfless love of Christ.

Editor of *Buzz*, Steve Goddard, found no fault in a Dylan who could say outspokenly to his record listeners and audiences 'when you gonna wake up and strengthen the things that remain?' Goddard felt that the middle-class people who heard Dylan preferred to hear the old Bob knocking the society that told them to desire, hold onto their possessions and consume. 'They can discuss the implications and nuances of each song as they drive home in their vinyl roofed Cortinas.' He felt the alternative Dylan was offering was not the one they wanted to hear.

In Britain's *Melody Maker*, Chris Bohn wrote that *Slow Train Coming* reeked of complacency, not contentment. 'It's devotion to Christ absolves it of all worldly responsibility,' he said but found some awesome and affirmative moments. *Contemporary Christian Music* saw the album concerned entirely with Dylan's new relationship to God and man. The magazine complimented the Jerry Wexler and Barry Beckett production at the famed Muscle Shoals studio and commended the authority of Dylan's vocals and the lean sinewy guitar work of Dire Straits musician Mark Knopfler. The writer saw Dylan standing foursquare against corruption, an advocate of righteousness.

In the journal *Firewind* (USA) Gord 'Flash' Wilson wrote 'Dylan's always used Biblical symbolism but now he believes it' – 'his forte is to relate what Jesus says to street and music people.' He expressed his joy when, switching on the radio, he heard the album's finale *When He Returns*, a slow gospel song with prominant piano and a hymn about Christ's coming. 'Once we dreamed of the day when gospel music would be on the waves, and we also prayed for Bob Dylan, but only God would connect the two.' Wilson's closing appeal was 'pray for our young brother, and dance in the street, all you middle-aged flower children – Bobby's home!'

Something of Wilson's joy was also caught by Tim Lenton in the British Christian weeklies – *British Weekly* and *The Church of England Newspaper*. 'To have this album at all is something of a dream come true. It could also unlock many a formidable door.' Lenton thought his influence would reach both young musicians and Dylan's contemporaries.

Saved and *Shot Of Love* were treated with slightly less, but still detailed, consideration. *Shot Of Love* started a new wave of speculation and gossip because it did not have the religious apocalyptism of *Slow Train Coming* nor the gospel feel of *Saved*. But such criticism was mild when compared with that following the release of *Infidels,* and to a lesser extent the album *Empire Burlesque* in 1985.

Some writers wondered what the criticism was about for to them *Shot Of Love* had plenty of sound biblical expression. They saw it saying quite clearly that man lived in a fallen world but with the ever present and the everlasting love of God. They suggested that those unfamiliar with Dylan's style had simply failed to recognise his use of irony. *Contemporary Christian Music* suggested he was involved in overall strategy and campaign against the forces of evil that few had bothered to understand and comprehend. They said 'the release of *Shot Of Love* is a blessed opportunity to see what an American artist and a man of God can do unhindered by current notions of what constitutes spirtuality in music.' Carl Pickhardt, keyboards man on the album, said, 'It's not as born-again sounding, lyrically, not images from the Bible and stuff, as much as just ordinary language that people in the street can relate to ... that's what the whole thing was about. Songs about life, but with Christ in the middle of it. Songs about what it's *really* all about.'

Infidels was a considerable change from the religiousness of his first two albums as a Christian and there was to some degree a return to the style and mannerisms of writing that characterised much of his early work. David Porter of *Third Way,* a British monthly journal, had some strong and perceptive comments to make. 'It's the music of a Christian, but a Christian who is too honest to conceal the fact that he is struggling with temptation, and too human not to make his confession with reticence . . . in the sixties and seventies Dylan's gift was to express on our behalf the pain of being human in an inhuman world. As a Christian, he has given us anthems, hymns and battle-cries. Now in *Infidels* he has portrayed on our behalf the perplexity of the Christian who knows the reality of the old man still active in his heart. It's a profoundly disturbing album expressing for us the pain of knowing that perfection is within us – but not yet. Too obscure for a confession, it's at least his prayer-letter. I hope it gets well read.'

It was not an album to excite the secular music press who gave it rather short shrift and suggested that Dylan had little left to say. To others *Infidels* said something about the freedom to spread the gospel naturally and powerfully without feeling a need to excuse that.

Undoubtedly Dylan's conversion had an incalculable impact upon the thinking and perceptions of thousands, possibly millions. Some may well regret that so much attention has been paid to secondary issues rather than to actually hearing and understanding what the man is now saying in his music. Many regret that his conversion has always been doubted and this has placed intolerable press-ures upon Dylan. Even some Christian writers could do well to remember Jesus' words about placing a millstone around the necks of the new believers.

Certainly the Dylan of *Infidels* and *Empire Burlesque* seems to have the mind of the Lord and his ideas accord with Scripture, even if he emphasises the uncomfortable challenges of the Gospel more than God's love seen in Christ. This emphasis has brought criticism.

Danny Smith wrote 'people have tried to second-guess Dylan' from the early times and they still do. He saw Dylan's faith reflected in some words he said to Robert Hilburn of the *Los Angeles Times* that 'where he was at' musically and spiritually, was captured on *Shot Of Love* – a statement of need, response and intent, of humility and vulnerability. Neither arrival nor departure, but something that rings genuine and true. Someone who's content to take time in the queue and isn't desperate to reach the spotlight.

The man has faith and we rejoice. Let's take the questions he asks seriously. What *are* we doing about being saved or being shot by God's love?

Soulsters

Philip Bailey

Younger pop fans know Philip Bailey as the singer who combined with Phil Collins for the massive hit single *Easy Lover*. Their record had constant airplay during the first part of 1985 and a video of the record constantly appeared on TV shows. It was one of those deceptive easy-sounding singles that at first hearing have little to them but in which one hears more and more with subsequent listening.

Easy Lover made the top spot. For Bailey it was an enormous factor in launching solo work and making a name for himself apart from Earth, Wind and Fire, arguably the most important U.S. black group in the 1970s. Christian fans were glad that here was a Christian at the top of his musical profession and someone who was not afraid to speak of his faith. Bailey was to record a solo album for religious label Myrrh under the title *Wonders of His Love*. He talked to music writers about music, God and Jesus, and they responded with respect.

In reviewing the Myrrh album one major reviewer wrote, 'Oh yeah. *That* Philip Bailey. The breezy, falsetto vocalist from Earth, Wind and Fire. So what does he sound like doing gospel music? Good, better and best.'

Knowledge of Bailey's career with Earth, Wind and Fire would have suggested that the Denver-born artist was well equipped to sing gospel. The famous American group achieved their fame through a wide variety of music. *Rolling Stone* magazine put it well, 'Their music is encyclopedic, topping Latin-funk rhythms with gospel harmonies, unerring horns, Philip Bailey's sweet falsetto and various exotic ingredients chosen by leader and producer Maurice White. Unlike their ideological rivals, the down-and-dirty but equally eclectic Parliament/Funkadelic, EW&F have always preached clean, uplifting messages.'

Bailey was not in the original group that White formed in 1969. Maurice had first formed an outfit from his experiences of the Chicago ghetto and joined with his brother Verdine who was adept at vocals, bass and percussion.

The band recorded one single for Capitol and two albums on Warner Brothers Records. A modicum of success came. White, son of a doctor and grandson of a honky tonk pianist, had worked with a number of artists before this. He had recorded with the Impressions and Muddy Waters and from 1967 to 1969 he was a member of the famed Ramsey Lewis Trio. Later he was to write the 1975 Lewis hit in the States, *Sun Goddess*. It was during this musical association that White established an interest in the African thumb piano, better known in some circles as the kalimba. It would soon be an essential ingredient of EW&F.

Philip joined in 1973 when White decided some changes were necessary. He wanted to improve the ideas that had originated during his days with Lewis but had not been fully exploited.

White too had strong church background. 'My grandma had had me singing in the sanctified church from the age of six but what I'd really wanted to do was to get into one of those drum and bugle corps because I liked their shiny uniforms so much.' Astrology rather than religion influenced his choice of name for the group; his chart has no water signs, hence the name.

Between 1966 and 1970 Maurice was with Ramsey on several trips to the East, and this is where his fascination with ancient Egyptian religion, astrology and other mystic sciences originated. 'My life started to change at this point,' he says and adds, 'I began studying under mystic masters and my consciousness was beginning to develop. I realised I had to begin relating more of my music to my generation so I split from Ramsey and went to Los Angeles.' His idea was to 'put together a band that would appeal to more than one group of people, and to more than one culture. Open up a whole new bag.'

The new group signed with US Columbia (CBS in the UK) and debued with *Last Days and Time*. There was brief chart action but far more influential in establishing the group was their second L.P., *Head To The Sky,* which was issued in August 1973. On the *Last Days and Time* album was a female vocalist called Jessica Cleaves plus Ronnie Laws and Ronald Bautista. This album saw White's introduction of the kalimba, now also familiar as the group's logo.

Open Our Eyes was recorded in the mountains of Caribou and maintained the high standard set. In America this album put two singles in the top 40, *Mighty Mighty* and *Devotion,* but it made no impression on the British listings although the group was becoming well-nown. There was a spiritual feel to the whole album and it had a Christian appeal although, in the final analysis, Christians would question the concept which White expressed in the words, 'In the group we draw all our forces from the universe and from the Creator and from the sky. This is where we're really coming from, we try to sound mystical because that's how we feel.' He listened politely but was not persuaded by my Christian viewpoint during an interview at this time. White was already into his generalised synthesis of religious beliefs.

In musical terms it all came together in 1975 when his brother Freddie joined the group and there was the tremendous success of the stunning album, *That's the Way of the World*. Philip Bailey was now the only surviving member of the 1972 line-up other than Maurice and Verdine.

By now their stage set had assumed a new dimension which partly reflected White's beliefs. There were objects resembling pyramids on stage and people kept disappearing. It was all very mystical.

The year 1975 was also marked by the splendid album *Gratitude*, and several singles. In America, *Shining Star*, *That's The Way Of The World* and *Sing A Song* were released. The British record buying public only took interest in EW&F 45s after *Saturday Nite* was a top 20 hit in 1977. The group subsequently had variable success in the British charts with ten records below the mid-twenties, but also some big ones such as *Let's Groove*, *After the Love Has Gone* and *September*. These three were also major US hits as was the top tenner *Got To Get You Into My Life* which only made 33 in the UK charts despite a lot of airplay. In 1976 the album *Spirit* was released and provided much of the material in their stage show that played ninety dates in the US alone. Pyramids, levitation and magic were amongst the attractions.

Of course this was not compatible with Christianity, but Philip wasn't a Christian at this time. He and Maurice shared a sense of the spiritual which could be detected on their seventh album, *All 'n' All*, released in January 1978. It was even more obvious on the next one, *I Am*; a great album by any standards. Maurice employed The Emotions for *Boogie Wonderland* which was successfully issued as a single.

Again I asked Maurice to comment on the inner source of the group's compositions. 'People try and describe us as a spiritual group. But you shouldn't confuse spiritual with religion. If people are tired of religion they shy away from us, we're not that, spiritual is something else that takes in the elements. What we are trying to do is instil confidence in people through our music.'

Philip Bailey, recalling those times, told Martin Wroe of *Strait,* 'Well originally the concept was of more than just a musical nature because we realised that musical ability is a gift from God and so we always wanted to do the music in a fashion which would be upstanding. There's so much bad rap about musicians – they're all supposed to be into drugs and the whole thing – so the group actually went about to try to destroy some of the myths about musicians. The message in the music was one of love and positive thinking.'

He pointed out that Maurice White was not the only person searching for spiritual experience. While Maurice pursued palmistry, Buddhism, astrology, pyramidology, mystical Egyptology, astrology and reincarnation others sought enlightenment elsewhere. Maurice never tried to enforce his beliefs on the others although the album sleeves often reflected his thinking. Yet of course he could not but unconsciously implant something upon those he worked with. But as Philip says with success after success resulting from the music, who was going to question the thinking behind it?

Phil experimented with Transcendental Meditation, Zen and became a vegetarian for a while. He still thought about Christianity occasionally, and remembered his Church teaching of his younger days. Yet he had never felt claimed by Jesus.

When he finally decided he would make a response to Jesus it seemed easy, yet provided no instant answers. He remembers praying a simple prayer. 'I prayed to God that if Jesus was the way, to reveal it to me.' Twelve months passed and the answer suddenly came with devastating impact. 'The world of God just pierced my heart and I began to weep uncontrollably. That night I knew beyond a shadow of doubt that Jesus Christ was real. I'd never experienced anything like that – it was like a flushing, that's the only way I can explain it. I felt like my sins had been washed away.'

He became firm friends with Leon Patillo and the Christian musician, formerly of Santana, took him through the Scriptures and showed him many wonderful truths. To Philip's great joy his wife also became a Christian. There were many questions to consider, one of the most pressing being whether he should stay in popular music and remain with Earth, Wind and Fire. Everyone offered conflicting advice and many pointed out the conflict of EW&F sleeves, Maurice's views, and some of the song lyrics with the precious truth he had now found.

Martin Wroe raised some of these points in his *Strait* interview. Phil told the music writer, critic and Christian, 'As for all the artefacts on the sleeves and the covers, and the signs and symbols ... the participation in astrology and all the things that Earth, Wind and Fire have pretty much been pegged to be about, one incentive to become vocal about my Christian beliefs is because I was continuously attacked as a Christian on the basis of all these things. I always have answered it the same way, which is the truth. Earth, Wind and Fire is Maurice White. Period. Stops right there ... all we do is the music. If the music is contrary to what we wanna sing we'll speak up but that hasn't happened.'

Philip's Christian faith was shared with a wider audience with the success of *Easy Lover* and the almost simultaneous release of *Wonders Of His Love*. There also was his solo album for CBS-Columbia titled *Chinese Wall*. It was clear that his spiritual growth had taken a different course from Maurice's. The sheer beauty of his voice and the simplicity and power of his songs really won the day. Britain's *New*

Music Express said 'If an angel could sing, he would probably sound like Philip Bailey.' Witter continued, 'It is a soaring, celebratory sound. It's the sound of a man who loves to sing.' He did not have much praise, however, for *Easy Lover* but it was subsequently successful and established Phil in his own right. Witter loved both the albums but seemed to feel *Chinese Wall* had a better sound.

'Stunningly well produced by Phil Collins, *Chinese Wall* is not only the most distinctive sounding soul album in recent years, it also blows away most of the competition in the pop arena. Bailey's "gospel album" is a church, operatic jazz-funk masterpiece, it showcases some of Bailey's most blissful singing, and proves conclusively that the devil doesn't have all the best tunes.' You can say that, again!

Bailey told Witter how his life had become full of joy and happiness, and his voice doubtless reflected this. 'It's an unprejudiced sound, because I relate to all sorts of people, and my belief in God, and that my voice is a gift, allows me to sing uninhibitedly.'

Witter told Philip: 'I love your gospel LP, and I get a lot out of it as an atheist, without having any interest or belief in the Christian message you're trying to convey. How do you feel about that?' 'I still love you!' he replied with a laugh.

The reviews in the Christian press were universally congratulatory. Britain's monthly *Buzz* chose it as a Record of the Month and their reviewer Tony Cummings praised it lavishly. In *Strait,* Graham Cray, an Anglican vicar with a great knowledge and awareness of rock and general pop culture history, thought it was the best album he heard for years that was released under a religious label imprint.

The album runs for forty minutes and is indeed packed with good things. The music is smooth and easy, an effortless but powerful testimony to Phil's voice and faith. Some of the songs have a direct evangelistic appeal, for example, *God Is Love* in which Bailey asks for a response from his listener and spells out the simplicities of the message. Jennifer Howes, joins him on this track. He has some amazing falsetto on the first side's finale *Safe In God's Love,* and indeed with backing reminiscent of a male choir, it could be a church setting, even an old-fashioned revival hour.

The second side is characterised by his ability to hit high notes and the ease with which he carries funk along with consistentlly clear delivery and emphasis. Here, as with *God Is Love* there is a sudden surprise ending, as this time a gospel choir replaces the solo voice. For a while it merely embellishes the music as Bailey goes through some arresting vocal gymnastics but then it goes with him as he stresses the song lyrics and then spells out the message. It can hardly fail to move! *The Wonders Of His Love* is familiar to many since he sang it at the 1984 Greenbelt Festival.

His album is personal, for listening on cans or for loud play where praise can be given as the record progresses. The title track could well have been placed after *Make Us One,* for the repetition of the title is indeed precious testimony and praise for the spirit-filled Christian.

Some critics felt it could have been less reflective and more social, although his splendid *Chinese Wall* met this demand. Among the album cuts is the moving *Children of The Ghetto,* the song that really brought the album into the US black music market, allaying fears that Bailey had succumbed to white pop. To him *Chinese Wall* represented a real chance to break the EW&F mould and he was not worried that it might surprise those expecting funky R&B. His first solo venture *Continuation,* was funky R&B and even with a studded cast including Sister Sledge, George

Duke and Deniece Williams, it had made little impact. It was simply accepted as a pleasant but ordinary R&B album. He wanted to avoid a repetition of this and also he had no desire to produce a record that might be regarded as a stop-gap EW&F release.

For Philip Bailey 1985 represented a time to break free. He could caress with his beautiful voice and present material with real class and style. He could do so as an established artist, he could afford to experiment and he could feel so many channels open to his words and message. For general record buyers Bailey's 1986 album was *Inside Out*. While, to a certain extent, his profile has diminished after the flourish of 1985, he continues to make thoughtful, quality soul music. As for Bailey, the person, he told Martin Wroe, 'The more people know I'm committed to Christ and I love Him the better ... hopefully they'll be inspired to search the Scriptures for themselves.'

How about it?

Steve Arrington

Disco records pour out of the pop machine with alarming speed in an effort to meet the dance floor market that demands different record titles, if not entirely new music, week in and week out.

More often than not, the record artist is secondary to the sound and even to the arranger, mixer, producer, and musicians. Some disco artists hardly sing a word or, if they do, they merely fill in between long spells of instrumentation. Words simply provide a chorus for the night people who dance life away in the make-believe world of the disco club.

However, the group Slave fared well in disco, R&B and black listings and in 1980 they danced their way into the pop Top 100 with *Just A Touch Of Love*.

Steve Arrington was important to the Slave line-up and sound. Their function was pretty straightforward – they provided music for dancing, and there was no real message in the music beyond 'have a good time'.

Arrington didn't complain. After all, he and the others were fast becoming heroes of black music people and getting their name known elsewhere. The money coming their way was useful and they could enjoy a higher class of living than many of their contemporaries.

Times were good, but once Arrington had savoured the initial good vibes he began thinking more closely about what he was doing. He was making good disco music but he wondered if there was an undue emphasis upon the sexual outside any context of love? Was there any point or purpose in merely being a mouthpiece for material that said little of lasting merit? What of himself? Wasn't being a media star, a club favourite, really illusory? Would the fans, the hypsters, DJs and drooling club and disco owners bother too much if Slave stopped making hit sounds? These were some of the questions that flashed through Steve Arrington's mind as he stood out there on the stage night after night or when he was interviewed.

Arrington had been raised in the Christian faith but as his dissatisfaction with his lifestyle grew he turned to search in other directions. He began eagerly reading and finding out about other faiths and was conscious of other black musicians whose interest ranged from astrology to scientology. It was a fairly enjoyable period of his life but increasingly perplexing, as his reading made apparent the vast number of systems that were options.

It was a personal mission that he soon shared with his wife India, knowing that whatever they found must be personal to each.

'My wife became very involved in this search of mine and she had her own journey to make. It's a help to know someone so very close is busily searching for a real meaning and purpose. She told me that I must hang on in there however I felt.'

Steve's life wasn't totally empty for there was respect and some admiration for his voice and music that sustained him a little. He knew there was more, however, something that would fulfil and satisfy in the long term.

He certainly couldn't find this in the pop culture. He took an interest in *The Wall* from Pink Floyd. The British super-group do not represent any religious sect but there is a pervading nihilism about their work that does effect and alter people's awareness.

Steve and millions of others sat and watched. He and

many emerged rather stunned by the coldness and emptiness around the film's message. There was no answer to life there, just a dead end and not a very pleasant one either.

He looked at the lives of fellow black artists including Marvin Gaye, a man with a definite religious background, a soul brother with a love for Jesus, yet ever conscious of his own inner failures, and insecurities. Gaye radiated intermittent musical genius, a warmth to fellow brothers and then there was the heavy drug taking. He seemed indeed a divided soul. When he was shot many felt that the inner man had been fighting for life for many a day.

'That man did so many beautiful things. He was a kind person. His album *What's Goin' On* was so powerful. He reached such heights and then there was this other side.'

While Steve appraised various schools of quasi-religious thought he also read the signs of the times and didn't like what he saw in the world. Man's behaviour, man's lack of respect for the world and fellow earth inhabitants appalled him. So did the decadence and the sense of lostness amongst young people including those closest to him, music fans.

'When I looked and what I saw – these things made me think – what is life? What was I doing that was positive? Yes, I could make music for I think music is neutral but then what would I do with my music? Just feed people with more empty songs?'

More reading and more searching followed but he found no real satisfying answers. Then a small incident on Broadway and 49th set Steve Arrington on the path towards finding real satisfaction.

'I was walking in New York with India. We saw one of those men carrying a banner and he was holding a placard that said "Jesus Is Coming".'

Most people pass on quickly or move off in another

direction rather than be confronted by such people, especially in New York. But Steve and India stopped, exchanged a few words, took some leaflets and went on their way with the placard headline reverberating behind them.

Steve recalled, 'I don't know, there was definitely something about this occasion. A whole lot of things had led up to this I feel. I really do. I felt so much emotion. I said to the man "Explain to me, now, what you are saying". I mean you don't in such places, I guess, but I wanted to. I don't even remember the time of day. Like I said, it was one of those moments when you felt at some kind of crossroads.'

On reflection, he admits it was ironic that after all the searching he in fact returned to the faith he had been taught as a child. Things were different now. He was really searching. He wanted something to satisfy his inner hunger. And he was finding the answer for himself.

'People can shout their faith to me but I have to know it for Steve Arrington period. That was me, at this time.' But what was it that Steve found this time around?

'The fact is this, out of all the religious figures I have ever heard of or listened to, read and thought about, Jesus is the only one to die and be raised from the dead. I thought how can one man bring us out of sin. Jesus came and died for us, even though we were sinners, and fell short of the life God wants us to live. It blew my mind! The fact of His love for us. The fact that we can gain heaven! Here we have the chance to gain the key of life. I mean we were born in God's image and we messed things up. But there's a way out of this. Wow!'

Steve talks of mans technological progress and adds, 'I mean, all that and we want to fight each other. There's the Middle East, Russian disputes, South America. And we don't understand ourselves!' Steve's first steps to a new understanding of Christianity initially felt strange, he seemed almost like a child once more; everything was new and fresh and exciting. 'I think you become very conscious of the immediate past life you've been living. Out there in the world you see things much more starkly and you see the insecurity of people so much more clearly.

'My uncle, Charles Cooke, was a preacher, so I had heard something of Jesus. It was part of my upbringing and in my youth I believed in God.' He hadn't really found a living faith in his childhood, however, but now, it was different. 'I felt a power in my life. To think I might have gone and found another faith. I had even enquired into spiritualism. But I think they take your mind. I think though you have to look around sometimes, have some options. And when you really find what you want then you can be really certain. So many avenues have been explored, and they've been found to offer nothing.'

It was a bold step for Steve to take, despite his religious background and the empathy of others in the business who were searching for something to give life some real meaning. Steve soon realised there were several major consequences arising from his decision. The first shock was recognising the need to tell others, including his audiences. To them Steve Arrington was a one-time member of Slave and known for nothing more than some good disco music which had a physical appeal.

'When you realise you've got to tell what has happened to you then you know you've made a bold step. People will be stunned and some will get all kinds of wrong ideas about you because of their wrong idea of what a Christian is.'

The second repercussion of his new committment was the need to redefine his approach to his future career. He could not talk of a new power changing his life and yet continue close involvement with a style of music that contradicted the very direction of that change.

Steve told his friends. Many were delighted, others uncritical but suspicious, waiting to see the fruits of the decision he said he had made. Telling the big wide musical world could wait for a while. He had no desire to become a media freak. The changes would be apparent when he launched his new musical career.

'I didn't want some kind of gimmickry to accompany my decision. I think you have to have a gift of discernment! I felt the time would be right when people were familiar with me, the solo artist with my own material and career forthcoming.'

It was not a cop-out. It seemed the best way and time has vindicated Steve's decision.

'People, I said, must know, they will know my decision. And I know they will want to check me out, to see the honesty of my move. But in my case there were those several things involved and far greater in their extent than most people might face.'

Arrington decided there was no need for a total change in his musical orientation – the feel for music that enables people to dance was ingrained in his consciousness, and he believed that there was tremendous scope in that line of music. He had thoughts of developing the music he had established on his first two solo releases but eventually he thought more in terms of albums. He produced *Dancin' In The Key Of Life* and simultaneously released the single *Feel So Real*. There was instant radio response to the single both in the UK and USA although the marketing efforts that backed the 12″ exceeded those for the single.

Suddenly Steve Arrington was news. *Feel So Real* had a sparkle and a gaiety that immediately caught the attention; one of those records that sent the listener scurrying to find about the artist. I felt that way and hearing this single sent me running to telephone the record company to know more of Steve Arrington and to ask for an interview. It was in conversation with Steve that I first learnt he was a Christian who talked of being born again, and on hearing the album I learned more of this musician's faith.

The album was recorded in Los Angeles and it marked Steve's first work with producers Keg Johnson and Wilmer Raglin. It was promoted by the record company as 'a multi-dimensional tour de force' opening in fine style with *Feel So Real*. The track had a R&B/pop/Latin blend, and there was extra zap from the tasty trumpet solo by jazzmaster Freddie Hubbard.

Steve Arrington found himself with a world audience. His single was airplayed everywhere. On the strength of the hit single there was radio play for the album and sales soared. He was chased by journalists and music writers who wanted to satisfy a sudden public demand for information on the artist behind *Feel So Real,* and *Dancin' In The Key Of Life*.

Steve clearly interpreted the lyrics of both songs in the context of his Christian beliefs although both could be understood in a secular light. In interview situations Arrington did not mince his words. He ignored the possible commercial disadvantages of speaking so openly of his Christian faith and said what he felt and knew. He believed he could proclaim his faith and keep his commercial appeal. He was proved right, a fine example to those who keep quiet about their beliefs for fear of harming their careers.

Steve said the album was almost a 'concept' with a definite theme. 'I don't think black artists as a whole have been into concept albums though there are some, for example albums from Marvin and The O'Jays.

'My linking theme is the reality of the Gospel — you don't have to sing religious words, you can portray the Gospel through direct lyrics and an evolving story line in songs showing clearly that the Gospel is needed.'

Underlying everything a basic professionalism established his high standards. 'I'm not into gimmickry. I make music for dancing but I want to say something as well, not just a kind a of "get-up-and-dance" shallowness. I want people to get familiar with my music, knowing that behind it there is something positive. Today there is so much decadence and artists like Prince and Madonna, well, what can I say? I want to be part of a pop movement that has some value.'

Steve could find a niche for himself in the large American religious music market but his chosen arena is the general music scene.

'Maybe I shall make an album of specifically religious songs. Fine. Then I may not. I see myself where it's all basically happening, the place where I can reach people who are being confronted by artists and songs that speak harm.'

Arrington sees his music being heard by people who are in a similar situation to the one he was in before his conversion. For, as his songs proclaim, and as he underlines in conversation, too many people search for meaning today, but finally choose decadence as the way out. He is concerned by lax morals and a lack of awareness that there are God-given laws by which we should live.

'I say on my album I've found the Lord and that no-one has to be alone in this universe. You have to hear his call. A lot of people don't know anything about it, it's not a popular thing.

'There is no point and no reason to be lukewarm about faith. If someone hadn't had enough enthusiasm to be out there walking on the streets then who knows, I might not have found what I have. I've been given a gift, the gift of God's love. I can give people the gift of music and more than that, I can offer them the gift of God's Son.'

Sister Sledge

Four vivacious girls rushed out of the hotel foyer and approached the black London taxi that was waiting. The driver waved his arms to indicate that the cab was not for them. He said he was waiting to collect a nun, Sister Sledge.

The girls collapsed in mirth and explained that *they* were Sister Sledge, a soul group from Philadelphia, USA. The cab driver could be excused his mistake; less excusable was the BBC DJ who, on giving the singles chart countdown announced *Frankie* was number one and then thundered 'she's made it'.

For the Sledge girls it was the summer of summers. Chart toppers do not come every day – it was their first number one and they had been charting in Britain since the gutsy *Mama Never Told Me* in 1975, a real rouser of a party number. Three Dog Night stole their thunder in the States but later they were to score high in their homeland and they accumulated a run of hits in Britain also.

Frankie was hardly a soul number – more a pop tune with a catchy air. Frankie himself could have been anyone but the girls said the original Frankie in the mind of songwriter Denise Rich was Frank Sinatra. The song almost never made their album *When The Boys Meet The Girls*. It came in late and initially made little impression upon them. Their producer, the famous soul man Nile Rodgers, was also unimpressed, it seemed so plain and ordinary. Record buyers later discovered the disc's hypnotic quality but fortunately Nile Rodgers did so a great deal sooner. He couldn't get it out of his head! He came back to the girls and announced with a wry smile that he had changed his mind. 'I can't stop singing the song, you've got to record it' he said.

To some people the song seemed an uncharacteristic choice for the group although that impression might not arise from observing their live work. On stage the girls showed straightforward commercial soul appeal, ready to rouse and excite their audience. In cabaret, however, the girls performed songs that demanded a wider range of musical abilities. *Frankie* seemed to fit this latter category but after it succeeded as a single it could be performed, and was demanded, everywhere.

The girls say *Frankie* is a lot easier to perform than many soul numbers. They like the element of fun. But its release was taking a chance. We thought – in the end – it was either going to make it or it would turn out to be one great disaster! It was so different from other releases. We don't know about it being a one-off, it was cute and it was a change. So you take the chance and then wait and see! This time it was worth sitting around and waiting. It was tremendous really because we were in Britain when it charted to the top. We called it "instant" action for audiences because we could go onstage and perform a number one there and then. Usually when something like that happens you're thousands of miles away.'

The album had nine tracks and it saw them reunited with Nile Rodgers, the producer responsible for their smash *We Are Family* album which was successful two times round thanks to the double charting of the title track. The album carried a number of songs which they featured alongside *Frankie* for their UK tour in the early summer – titles like *You're Fine, Hold Out Poppy, Following The*

Leader and *When The Boys Meet The Girls*. Several of the songs were written by Kathy and Joni.

Frankie's chart topping was the climax to several years of hits that had come, in part, from fresh mixings of old hits starting with *Mama Never Told Me* in 1975. The future had seemed bright. The pop papers ran the features. Sister Sledge was touted and recommended. Then came silence. The mysterious deadening reaction which happens to many singers who have one hit and expect others but never find them coming their way. There was no further chart life until 1979 when the group began a succession of high-class singles consistently characterised by their exuberance and life. *He's The Greatest Dancer* was a top ten hit both sides of the Atlantic. It had a lightness and an effortless style; the words tumbled over a catchy beat and the title line lodged in the mind in much the same manner as *Frankie*.

We Are Family was close behind it, in fact even before *He's The Greatest Dancer* disappeared out of the British top 50 people were humming, swaying and singing to *We Are Family*. For Americans the song caught something very precious to their way of life. Again the song had an engaging feel, warm and friendly, and that extra, elusive ingredient that makes a mighty smash hit. You felt their family was part of all families, the family of man that could exist off its own inner generosity.

For some inexplicable reason the girls could not make the Top 40 back home. In Britain, they were still loved and wanted. How could it be otherwise with a song such as *Lost In Music,* that haunting number that could hypnotise anyone in love with music. The girls blended beautifully with the music. It was not so successful in the charts as *We Are Family,* which had reached number eight but it made the top 20. Then after two other hits came a further unexplained lull. There was *Got To Love Somebody* and an infectious, good title-riffed song called *All American Girls*. The latter was another song – like *We Are Family* – which in concert can be sung with arms linked, hips swaying and an overall joyous air.

Thankfully the barren chart season ended and in May 1984 the girls were back – and how. A string of hits followed. A really gorgeous disco-tailored number began the new era of hitsville Sister Sledge. First, there was *Thinking Of You*. When they sing this on stage it becomes extended in the joyous celebration of love. The next two hits saw the return of oldies but now they were freshly mixed and given a backing that was contemporary with the disco feel of the year. These two hits were *Lost In Music* and *We Are Family*.

The girls insist that they were never far away from the big-time during the period when the pop charts failed to list their songs. Debbie makes the point strongly and firmly. 'The albums did well during this period of no pop hit singles. In America they reached the top of the rock'n'roll chart but somehow tracks were not picked up by the pop programmes and others. It has a lot to do with marketing.' Perhaps so, yet it would also be true to say that their material wasn't quite so strong during this period.

Nile Rodgers was the remix reviver of *Lost In Music*. He was one-half of the famed US, Chic Organisation. The other member was Bernard Edwards who had been responsible for the *We Are Family* album first time around.

It was Rodgers who agreed to produce the next album, which they hoped would consolidate their come-back, and, of course, thanks to *Frankie* it did.

But Nile had caused a few problems for the girls! They were versed in singing the songs as they had recorded them first time around. It wasn't so easy adapting themselves to fit the clever snipping and editing of the producer. Kathy told Paul Sexton of Britain's music weekly *Record Mirror* of one of the embarrassing situations for them.

They were in Britain and had turned up for a PA at Gulliver's club. They found *Tossing And Turning* had been chosen as the track by which they would get the audience happy, but alas, Nile had rather played around with the original version.

'Nile took a lot of Joni's ad lib lines, and on some of those lines she's actually repeating herself now. It was really hard, she had to study the record a lot. Because one thing we stuck to is doing the record the way the audience knows it.

'*Thinking Of You* wasn't even in our show, we had to add it. Kim and I really loved the song; it was a real sleeper.' But while they're grateful for the skills of Rodgers or Edwards the girls keep a firm hold on other aspects of their career.

Along with their manager 'mum' they keep a careful watch on their image. The girls insist they are not into a tacky image and they are not interested in being sex objects. When Paul Sexton interviewed them on another occasion for *Record Mirror* they told him, 'We have everything to do with our image. The album was originally going to be called *Dancing On The Jagged Edge,* that's one of the most popular songs on it. So for the photo session we all dressed accordingly and looked very rough and tough. Then the title got changed to *When The Boys Meet The Girls* and with the way we look, it looks as if we're saying when the boys meet the girls, there's going to be a war! It's funny how these things happen.'

As for the sexy image, Kathy told Paul, 'We don't really try to promote sex or push it, we don't wear low cut dresses or go out with nothing on. Someone was asking me if we push sex and I said no, but sometimes we come across sexy.'

For Sexton the girls are simply entertainers, though he notes, 'with producers like Nile Rodgers around Sledge will always be liable to make the rhythm a bit more dangerous. Kathy says she'd still love to work with Thomas Dolby and I don't see him making them sound like "Stars on Sunday".'

When freedom from pregnancy allows, the girls are fitness fanatics. When they came to Britain in the autumn of 1984 they brought a trainer along with them. He knocked on their bedroom doors regularly at seven in the morning and issued a command to get going! They ran for around two miles each time and then did a forty minutes aerobic class.

However, the greatest factor in keeping them together has been their lasting religious faith. It's something that is always with them. It's at the centre of their attitude towards and direction in life.

They were raised in the Christian faith. Gran is a staunch Baptist while dad is a Methodist minister. As kids it was axiomatic they went to church to give praise each and every Sunday. The girls went to both churches! Kim told me at one of our meetings, 'Does it matter? I think what is important is that we are all Christians.'

Unlike some stars who abandon their Christian up-bringing once they become independent and get caught by the lure of materialism, the girls have retained their faith. Kim tells me that their faith is the most precious thing they have and that without it they would have floundered a long time ago.

'You know in this business it's easy to go off the rails and you can get very despondent sometimes, even disillu-sioned. There are all kinds of people who think no further than the next buck. We have made money but it is secondary at the end of the day.'

She talks with animation of their faith sustaining them

daily. 'We pray each day. We have our Bibles with us. And we keep in contact with the Church. Whenever we can we get to Church. Too often we're in a plane or whatever but that can't stop us reading our Bibles. You have to keep in contact with God!'

She explains further what she means when she talks of the importance of finding God's will and she stresses, 'Prayer is everything, it was a great experience just finding that. It means a lot in our family. So many things come our way and you have to practice what you preach in those situations.'

Kim says she is aware that, whatever some people might say, a pop star does exert considerable influence on fans. She knows fans watch what they do and what they say. She is particularly alert to what is happening in the music world and she talked briefly, on one occasion, to me about the amazing selling album *Thriller* and the accompanying video.

'We've worked with The Jacksons and I know Michael. They are friendly people. But when *Thriller* came out I was worried. In a way it didn't say much but it was a horror movie and it played on horror. I'm not too sure what my reaction is other than one of being cautious for I think it may portray some aspects of life that are not good.'

But she has no doubt about the life-style of another American heart-throb of the eighties – Prince. 'It's pretty bad stuff. *Thriller* didn't endorse evil or drugs but with someone like Prince it's all – well, it's blatant and I don't like the statements being made.'

It's not easy in pop either to find time to relax or have normal companionship. But a faith can be vital and for Kim the Christian faith has underpinned and nourished her life. This is true for the others, as well. Debbie speaks of the valuable family background that they've had and she distinguishes carefully between casual acceptance of a belief obviously found useful, and possessing a faith that is based on a personal acceptance of Jesus as Lord and Saviour. She remembers the great moment when she said 'yes' to His claims and went racing to tell her sisters. They all fell on their knees and gave thanks. She says she knows a great many people are raised in a religious framework but drop away and are never encouraged to make a personal commitment. Their faith is second-hand.

She respects those young people who learn to ask questions and who make an effort to finds answers rather than sit back, taking what may or may not come their way. She is aware that constant travel can interrupt the best of personal schedules, that demands are increasingly made and particularly so when the popularity stakes are high, as happens when there is a record charting. Sometimes she is so exhausted that she is glad she is driven to depend on God, times when she realises her own frailty and equally His goodness. At other, less traumatic times she has her sisters and, of course, her husband.

For Debbie it's sad that so many people do not bother with religious faith, more so when a great mass of young people are desperate for something real, so real as Steve Arrington might say! She can only testify herself and say 'He never leaves nor forsakes' and be aware that though she may slip away 'He is there waiting for us to return.'

It's something to which all the girls shout 'Hallelujah', and why not!

David Grant

It was one of those marvellous musical marriages that happens every now and then. A re-make of the old commercial soul number *Could It Be I'm Falling In Love* gave David Grant and Jaki Graham a top five single. It sounded better than the original with a magic all of its own and the vocals had an exuberance that never infected the original version by The Detroit Spinners.

David Grant said it was simply, 'Corn, corn, corn all the way. I dreamt about us singing it, I really did. Then when I woke up and thought about it, it really made sense, I couldn't understand why no one had ever done it before. The song just seemed to split up really well for a duet.'

Paul Sexton in Britain's music weekly *Record Mirror* was right when he wrote, 'Wasn't it a bit risky covering a song that's so fondly recalled by so many people?' David responded, 'Well, a lot of people have been saying, "Hmm, doing a cover, isn't that the easy way out?" But if you think of all the covers that come out during the year that never even get heard because they're so bad – it's more difficult. We didn't try to make it sound modern. We just wanted to do it because we loved the song so much.'

He told Paul that to him it was one of those nostalgic songs that take people back to a certain time and place where they remember exactly what they were doing. 'That's partly because it came out before the video thing, and people formed their own images from it.'

The record gave Jaki, born in Birmingham of Jamaican

parents, her first real taste of fame. For David it was another rung on the ladder towards recognition as a major black British artist.

He had started his career as a record reviewer on a North London paper then joined Island in their press office. He had lent his promotional energies and skills to bands like The Wailers (Bob Marley's old band), Hi Tension and Third World, but was simply a stop-gap until he could realise his own musical ambitions. Around 1978 things began to gel. He met a guy called Sketch and they formed Linx. David was 20 at the time. Two years passed before anyone showed any interest and then it was only because they took the initiative and really put their money where their mouths were.

They scraped some money together, recorded *You're Lying,* and had enough small change left to have a 1,000 copies pressed. Then they had to sell and promote the record! They toured shops and tried to find friends who had friends who had mates in the radio stations. It was day-to-day living. It was hard but later, with success behind them, they saw it as fun. It was a good record and DJs were attracted, some by the sound and others by the thought that they could later claim to have 'found' a new outfit that would be big.

Chrysalis, a major company off London's Oxford Street with a bevy of star names associated including Ultravox, Michael Schenker, Billy Idol, Paul Hardcastle and Go West, thought Linx had something, at least the record did. They re-issued it under their umbrella and so gave it the benefit of professional promotion. Their confidence was justified, for it hit the British top 20.

David and Sketch were thrilled. Linx was to have another five hits. *Intuition,* which sold some 200,000 copies in the States, *Throw Away The Key, So This Is Romance, Can't Help Myself* and *Plaything.* But although they had a fair number of hits there was a struggle to get really high, though *Intuition* reached seven and *So This Is Romance,* 15. *Throw Away The Key* hit 21 but the last two were short-lived affairs at the lower end of the chart and together they spent three weeks apiece in the top 75.

Perhaps it was inevitable the two would call it a day and the talented David would try his luck as a solo artist. There was no real difficulty initially in attracting interest from the record people. His voice and face were known.

It took David some six months to decide where he might go musically. It was a new and strange experience to be out there, on his own. At least, it was a challenge. Eventually he recorded an album and from it came a veritable collection of hit singles. One of them, *Watching You, Watching Me* made the top ten. But things went quiet soon after this flourish and only picked up again when he joined forces with Jaki.

This amazingly energetic girl had sung for years in clubs and she had sung back-up vocals for a number of artists and groups including Landscape and UB40. It was Jaki's vocals which backed UB40's big hit *Many Rivers To Cross.* They met when his manager took David to hear her sing with the Medium Wave Band at Ronnie Scotts.

'My manager had said, "She's great, but she doesn't know she's great." After I saw her, I said, you've got to sign her. I went backstage to see her and said, "You're great!" She said, "I'm trying".'

Jaki is so vibrant and alive that only the dullest and saddest could fail to be enlivened by her presence. She relentlessly comes at you with a mix and laughter. The duet with David set her career in a new light. It meant there was considerable interest in any future recording. They decided they should not become known as a duo nor rule out the possibility of future collaboration. But Jaki was free to launch out and make real use of material she had previously recorded. She had released two singles *What's The Name Of Your Game* and *Heaven Knows (Feels So Good)* with the latter almost making the British top 40 singles. These two singles enabled her to find an album deal with EMI and it was with this company that she found her big chart triumph during July 1985, *Round And Around* and huge popularity for the 1986 hit *Set Me Free*.

A mum with a young daughter, Jaki found sudden solo success rather tiring. She was regularly off to London and back for recording, record company business and the inevitable round of media interviews. But at least she was going places. As she told me, 'I may never get this chance again and I've got to take it.'

It was partly her producer Derek Bramble who had got her where she was, both with David and on her own. 'I had sung but no one said to me, you can do this or that note. I just say "Yes, man" and I go high and make it! But Derek also says "you must be what you feel". Not many people tell you that. He's made me do things that I thought I could never do.'

Jaki professes no deep religious belief. 'David has, not me. Well, I'm not anti-religious if you know what I mean. I go to church sometimes but I don't take it seriously like he does. I think we've all got our own beliefs; no, I can't take it the way David does. He gets very involved.'

She is well aware of David's commitment and knows he will gladly share his faith if she wants him to, for he has not hidden his faith away. He came from a Christian family and learned early that each person must make their own commitment and that the role of the church is far from purely social.

He went to church with his parents in Hackney, East London. David was born in Jamaica and came to Britain at the age of three. His church-going carried less and less conviction as he grew and it was not until he had his first hit record with Linx that he began to search for some meaning in the teaching of his childhood.

He remembers his first singing days in front of his school class with fondness, even singing for his mum and driving the neighbours crazy! Even his mates at Boys' Camp received the Grant vocal treatment. At school he realised that his voice so charmed his teacher that he was let out a few minutes early and that meant 'I'd be at the ice cream van and playing football before anyone else!' Later in his career when that charm no longer worked he took lessons from a New York vocal coach who worked with the likes of Patti Labelle and Luther Vandross.

These days he is an active member of the Arts Centre Group. He thinks it great that Christian artists can join together and find time to share the faith that is so precious to them. 'Christian artists are very scattered and they don't meet up too much. I think it's fine that something like the ACG can bring people together.' Artists on tour have real problems becoming part of any community of Christians, so a base with a group of people who understand is very precious.

David has learnt that all the personal success in the world does not guarantee inner happiness. He tells of his elation at gaining a hit record and his delight with the television appearance which followed and the attention of the music press. He thought the world was his and he says he was suffering under the delusion that recognition would change everything. He thought life would become doubly and trebly happy. But he soon realised how transitory it can all be in the world of show business. Today's star can be tomorrow's has-been.

Contact with some Christians led him to a personal faith. 'I recognised that I need Christ and I believed. God became more important to me than anything else.'

He told Nick Beggs in Nick's book *Nick's Mix*, 'I'd

had problems before because I felt the church didn't understand me and I was inclined to condemn them because they were different. Now I realised this was an immature way of looking at it. In fact, God is a God of individuals, he doesn't treat us all the same.' And Dave, talking with me, said, 'My strength comes from my faith. Music is my contact with people. I'm not a speaker, that kind of thing. I don't find it easy to get thrown in front of an audience and then talk.'

Working out his faith in practical terms, David has been concerned about sickle cell anaemia, a disease that hits young black people causing deformities in the blood cells. With Errol Brown of Hot Chocolate and British first division football player, Garth Crooks, he has organised fund raising events and concerts to make money available for research.

He is also concerned with the inevitable problems faced by many black people in society. He is concerned that many of them feel rejected, unwanted and regarded as dispensable. 'I want to see black kids walk tall, so I want to support voluntary centres where black kids can get support and have the feeling that they are wanted, but it's not easy.'

He has a love for gospel music but while several gospel choirs have made the the pop charts, David believes basic funk is more accessible to millions. 'I think R'n'B and funk is the music of the streets. I think black groups are coming through strongly, even in Britain. It's not just the US who have the good bands.

'I do try and get involved with some of the young gospel choirs and I know some of the North London ones. The Gospel is important to me, don't misunderstand. I see Philip Bailey is doing well. He's been big with Earth, Wind and Fire and now he's having solo success. You see I feel he can make so much more impression because he's reached there as an artist. I think what I can say can be so much more powerful if I say it through my own style of music. What is more natural?'

He believes the general music scene has real creative potential, whatever the musical idiom. However, he is aware of its less savoury aspects and that the predominantly financial goal of the pop world causes inevitable problems.

He loves music and he adores his role as a singer. It's a world he does not take lightly. He told Paul Simper of UK pop journal *No. 1,* 'It's not the way I look or dance. It's the way I sound.'

But he does look good; he's a cool, snappy dresser and never fails to take care of himself. He always looks lithe, slim, and many – including *No. 1* magazine – have noted that he radiates confidence and purpose.

Paul remarked, 'David's got many reasons to be cheerful'. He problably meant those solo hits and the successful partnership with Jaki but David can add his faith. Because he truly believes that there is a God, reason for his existence and music. He told me: 'I really love it where I am and I feel I've been led by God.'

Paradise

'Feeling a little tired and listless? The strain of daily survival telling? Need a relaxing holiday in some balmy tropical resort but can't afford it?' So read the announcement of a new Paradise single on the record label Priority. The record was *One Mind Two Hearts*. Throughout Britain disco clubs had been alerted by generous supplies of a white 12". Paradise had become news for producing a class pop-soul record and the group was being compared with greats such as Earth, Wind and Fire, Average White Band and George Benson.

The excitement was intense for there has been a long search in Britain for a lasting soul outfit. There have been a few fairly successful British black groups but somehow along the way the momentum always died. Now for Paradise big things were promised.

Paradise came riding in on the gospel momentum that had affected the British music scene of 1984. Their music had been heard by Christians in halls and concert auditoriums and they had appeared at the Greenbelt Festival and received ovations. Their appeal was seen beyond the gospel circuit and they had the quality to make a real impact on the pop scene. They were hot property, sought by record companies who queued for their signatures. Barry Evans, who became their producer-manager, had been aware of their growing potential over several years and after 1983 saw Paradise on the way to achieving success in the mainstream record market. When he signed them to Priority he believed it was now time to put the band's career into overdrive. The years of commitment had reaped dividends. Musically the result was a refreshing and unique mixture of superb, distinctive lead vocals, full smooth harmonies and a backing that had the feel, tightness and class of the best American sidesmen. It offered something fresh and vibrant compared with the mass of formularized music on offer in the black funk circles of the time, and particularly in the disco world that had become heavily reliant on the engineering and technology with the artist only allowed the occasional grunt or two.

As Schmaltz, the publicity company, proclaimed, 'Paradise are a much needed and guaranteed injection of musical sunshine into the worldwide music scene.' The group certainly had a natural joyous, infectious enthusiasm, and they wrote thoughtful and positive lyrics. Their appeal was a broad one.

The year 1983 proved to be a momentous one for the group. Their album *Love Is The Answer* was rapturously received and it was followed by several releases in the religious record market. The album title track was released as a single. They were nominated for a Gospel Grammy Award in the USA and in addition they were awarded the 'Best Group' and 'Best Vocalist' (in Paul Johnson) awards in a British Gospel Award event. At Greenbelt they won 25,000 fans.

The band numbered six, a hefty crowd for the tight economics of the music world. They were based in London. Sharp photographic readers always noticed 'eight' in their photographs! It was one of those crazy things! The guys said they were Christians and everyone knew it, but sheer talent attracted the loyalty of fans who might otherwise have been put off by the group's beliefs.

The band received the enthusiasm of the record world with commendable caution. Endless words have been spoken in times past of countless groups and singers who have finally come to nothing. In pop-land groups come and they go – fast. After all, only a handful of records chart in Britain each week from a release schedule of some 100 or more. Paradise members were aware of this. Underlying and shaping their ambitions was a strong Christian faith. They did not have the support of some black churches which were against Christian involvement in the pop world but they believed they were being honoured by God.

Paul told me on one occasion, 'It's really fantastic. He has given us a marvellous opportunity to witness. No way are we some kind of divine messengers but we are utilising the talents He has given us.' It was a view shared by Junior Edwards. The bouncing beaming Junior said, 'There is something special in what is happening. We are being blessed. We are black but we are part of a mixed community and we can relate to both black and white – doesn't the Christian faith do just that?'

Junior added, 'We have Christian material. And we're not just into marketing anything. I don't know, really . . . Others have tried to chart gospel and failed but we're there! Our song is about our faith and our relationship with God but we have to spell it out and we do so in interviews. But we can't stop people initially thinking it's a boy-girl love number.' The song was *One Mind, Two Hearts*.

Junior said he was determined that the group would help rid the soul-funk world of mindless lyrics which, Junior says 'go on and on about boogie down and your troubles away' and provide no answer for anyone.

He spoke of his admiration for an artist like Cliff and said he knew there was some sorrow and heartache ahead for the group because some people would misunderstand their motives as much as they often accused Cliff of using his gospel work to sell records!

'I think some see me as a backslider and all of us sometimes wish we had more support. But we think we have a positive image and we tell people the good news!'

When I spoke with them they did not know of my own Christian faith and witnessed to me without feeling embarassed or awkward – it seemed the most natural thing in the world, which is how it should be!

Paradise had other singles, including a lovely version of the Lennon-McCartney number *We Can Work It Out*. Through the early part of 1984 they played clubs and had a number of headlining events at major venues. But by summer 1985 Paradise was not where they had hoped to be. Lead vocalist Paul Johnson left when he found his recording commitments and live shows with Paradise conflicting with his work in the London Community Gospel Choir. It was an amicable split. Since then Paradise has found their first white member Belfast-born Paul McClements, previously with Nick Beggs in Kajagoogoo. The new team released the record *Heartstrings*. Its infectious dance rhythm set many feet a-dancing. By now Paradise had become a foursome, with Junior Edwards, bass; Philip Edwards, keyboards; David Aieyola, guitar and Paul on vocals.

Perhaps by the time you read this, Paradise will have arrived in a big way. If not, no matter, for while pop fame can come and go the presence of their Lord lasts for ever. That right, Junior?

Donna Summer

Misunderstanding came Donna Summer's way in 1975 when she became the sultry sexual temptress of soft-porn pop. The saga started when she moaned and groaned her way through a British-American pop smash *Love To Love You Baby*. Its airplay was restricted to times when only those of responsible years are expected to listen although the subject of the song was hardly unusual in the history of pop. What made the record different was that it simulated twenty-two orgasms that largely consisted of moaning and groaning which roughly transcribed was 'Ooooh, aaah, love to love you, bay-bee'. *Newsweek,* the famous US magazine, said it made Donna disco's 'First Lady of Lust.' The same thought seemed to grab hold of endless writers and journalists and she became one of the most talked about and sought after artists of the late 1970s. Her name, her picture, her story ws everyone's. Her profile was spread across magazines ranging from teenage pop to *Penthouse*. Even the regular press paid her attention. She was told by the *New York Times* that she was 'disco's artistic coming of age' and that she spins the Cinderella tale of a girl 'who lived in a land of dreams unreal/Hiding from reality'. Donna said some of those who wrote and published were trapped within their own world – 'it was mostly autobiographical.'

While kids danced to the pulsating feel of *Love To Love You Baby,* and the public read journalists' outpourings, the lady herself began to feel 'I was like Marie Antoinette or

Joan of Arc – great women of their time who had to deal with ridicule and misunderstanding'. She was being crucified on the altar of sales, but she was hardly the first to suffer this fate nor would she be the last. The record was hardly a bad disc, in pure pop commercial terms it was a blinder and in its entirety one of the most powerful dance concoctions ever to find its way on to vinyl, for all its blatant sexuality.

Donna had needed a hit. While she had achieved some limited local fame she was still just another good-looking girl with undoubted potential that was only a minor qualification in an industry that created its own. In show-biz terms she was fortunate to be chosen to front a 'sound' that could have been made by anyone really. And the market, with the growing disco orientation, was characterized by the fickleness of DJs, dancers and the buying public who demanded the next new thing almost before it was available and certainly before they were commercially available to the great mass of singles buyers.

It was a world where omnivorous dancers leapt about and the degree to which they switched, twitched and filled or emptied the disco floor could determine the eventual interest of companies. Some record concerns would even drop scheduled releases if the advance plays did not impress the patrons.

As *Rolling Stone* put it, Donna on *Love To Love You Baby* became 'a servile vixen with a whispery voice, intoning and moaning over a metronomic beat that had all the intensity of a sex act between consenting androids!' But it made her a household name worldwide and put behind her for ever the days when she was a filing clerk trying for a hit in a Munich studio.

Donna Summer was in reality Donna Gaines, one of seven children born to a Boston tradesman and his school-teacher wife. Six of the seven kids were girls and they and their parents lived in a three-family house. 'I had to compete. To be heard, you had to talk loud. Either that or you just tried to find an empty corner where you could sit and fantasize about being some place else. School wasn't any easier. I went to school with some pretty violent people, and I was an outsider because I couldn't live on that black-and-white separatist premise.'

She also went to church and learned of God, Jesus and the power of the Gospel to bring new life. She caught something of personal miracles and heard testimonies to the ever-present power of God in people's lives.

She heard the greats like Mahalia Jackson and Dinah Washington. She knew she wanted to be an artist and she had a gut feeling that she would be famous, one day. But she knew that the road to success would be littered with pitfalls and it was so, at the outset. She joined a group but they had hard drugs running alongside and helping their music. It didn't help theirs or her body but even if they couldn't see it, she could. She left and journeyed elsewhere.

She auditioned for the Melba Moore part in the Broadway musical *Hair*. She won and toured Europe with the company in one of the musicals of the age. She was part of the *Hair* cast in Munich, Germany and when the show closed she remained and married an Austrian member of the cast Helmut Sommer. They later divorced.

She appeared in a number of musicals, and to earn some more money and widen her horizons and contacts she sang back-ups for recordings in the Musicland Studios, much favoured by many Western artists as an ideal setting to create the sound they wanted.

In Munich she met producer Giorgio Moroder co-owner of the Oasis label with Pete Bellotte. She recorded a number of singles for Oasis. Neil Bogart's Casablanca label picked up a distribution deal with Oasis and eventually released *Love To Love You Baby*. It was Bogart who once said 'I used to tell people to take Donna home and make love to her – the album, that is.'

So, the record made her a winner, a massive selling artist and the discordant voices that condemned its sexuality only fuelled the enormous public interest. It was a rerun of the 1969-70 saga of *Je T'Aime* from Jane Birkin and Serge Gainsbourg.

The single heralded a career of smash hits. There was a nine-month lull when the record dropped from the charts after a three-month run from the end of 1975. Her titles flooded the market and were partly helped in Britain by the fact that two companies owned different material and issued competing discs. They all sold well.

The constant flow of success silenced her critics. It was admitted, slowly and almost grudgingly that she did have a voice after all and that she was not capable of only embellishing the creation of producer/engineer and the fertile imagination of the creators of sexual fantasy. Her hits included such titles as *I Feel Love, Last Dance, I Love You, Love's Unkind, I Remember Yesterday, Rumour Has It* and *Back In Love Again*.

Her market penetration continued unabated in the last three years of the 1970s. Some sixteen titles charted in the British top 75 and only one, *Last Dance,* failed to make the top 40. In America, nine releases made the magical 40, and she had eight top 50 albums in Britains between 1976-9. It was quite a feat.

On the whole the sexuality was subtle. Sometimes it was blatant, particularly the tacky arresting cover of *Bad Girls* with its hooker imagery. She told people 'I have an incredible ability to fantasise. I'm undersexed, actually I am sensual and very physical. I'm very erotic. But my sexuality exists on a sort of fantasy level.'

She expressed some of her fantasies and hopes in an assortment of journals including some adult publications, though they were hardly hard-core pornography. She told of receiving explicitly sexual letters and was often asked to account for her following in the homosexual community. She answered, 'I think I have a strange kind of earthiness that might be alluring for a man who isn't into women sexually.'

Somehow she brought her religious beliefs into her situation. She was not yet a Christian but she did believe her life had some kind of purpose, that 'God gave me a reason to be here.' Donna in 1979 simply meant 'I think there is life after death and that everyone has a karmic debt to pay back; and whatever that is, I want to pay back before I go. I must have made some Christians wince.'

When the 1980s dawned she had a new contract with Geffen and then Warner Records. She was given quality material of a more varied nature. Soon she would be singing songs with a powerful religious undercurrent and some of them would specifically tell of her new-found faith and commitment to Jesus. She developed artistically and her life-style was a remarkable turn-around. For journalists it heralded an era of fresh copy! Among those with whom she was to work on record was the talented Christian Michael Omartian. She also worked with Matthew Ward, of the remarkably talented Christian recording trio Second Chapter Of Acts.

When Donna looked back and recognised the satanic influences that had often pervaded and controlled her life she cringed. Some of the things she had done appalled her. 'In Hair we would sing this song called *Me And Lucifer, Lucifer And Me*. Think about that – me and the Devil!' It gave her a real understanding of people who become trapped by Satan and enslaved to sin and a greater sympathy and love for those who find themselves weighed down by life's problems. 'The devil tries to take away people focusing on God,' she said.

Her examination of her past made her realise the mess she was in. In career terms she was extremely successful with a future that few had predicted when she burst upon the scene with *Love To Love You Baby*. But deep down she was a lost soul, even suicidal. 'I was taking medicine for stuff I should have been praying about!'

She had guilt for which she should have been asking forgiveness of God. But she had friends, pop stars who were Christians and an understanding minister friend. The pastor prayed with her and she felt the weight of her past lifted, and the anger and oppression of a diseased spirit was taken away. A new life dawned although she soon realised that people wondered whether the prodigal had really come home. Only time could heal and remove these doubts. She is not a theologican or a Bible scholar. She is someone with Christian experience that will be deepened within the circle of loving Christian friends. Some of her future work would be intended to counteract the old associations of lust and sexual pleasures.

The Donna who has emerged hasn't reduced her bubbling personality. She is out front strong and vibrant, capable of making mistakes and causing controversy. Her music has remained strong and firm, creative and addictive in a totally new way. Love is still a theme, for could there be popular music or life without it? But love is now God based with a different quality. The sexual element remains but as part of love overall, or its greatness and vastness, and not simply as a means of instant but short-lived satisfaction. Albums such as *The Wanderer, Donna Summer, She Works Hard For The Money* and *Cats Without Claws* are powerful moments and amongst songs of life and living there are strong testimonies to the supernatural love of God that enables her to shout on the later album, *I'm Free*. No longer a sultry temptress to be marketed as a product but a child of God to live in His light!

Deniece Williams

I had breakfast with Deniece in a London hotel. It was a friendly affair. We laughed a great deal. It was mid-morning cereal, toast and marmalade, for music people rise late with bedtime often in the early hours. And even when someone arrives in another country on a PA visit it's still hard to lose a habit they've formed from endless gigs and tours.

Deniece appeared fresh, attractive and bubbling with energy. It was a good time to meet her, for she was riding high at the top of the British charts with *Free,* which was faring in Britain far better than in her home country where it never passed the 20 mark.

The single was a glorious piece of soul pop that was vocalized as effortlessly as the title suggested. The song had some very high notes some of which were held for considerable periods. Everytime she wafted those thin notes into the air you felt that glass was in danger; if the radio or speakers were not turned down disaster would strike!

She began singing at an early age in church and had heard, loved and then sang gospel for herself. It had taught her rhythm, vocal inflection and an ability to handle varying tempos. She emphasised that while her own musical repertoire included gospel, it was wider, much wider. 'If I stopped at one kind of music then I would limit my growth as an artist. I sing gospel, R&B, pop, reggae and I'm developing an affection for country.'

She described herself as a lady of variety, and she said she resented those who demanded a narrow definition of her musical wares, so imposing limits on her work.

Her ambition at this time was simple to state but harder to achieve. She said, 'I would like to do with my voice what you can do with an instrument. I play the flute and sometimes when I've recorded my playing I've then over-dubbed my voice, so that I can relate it in sound, pitch and, most important, texture.'

She recalled her early life. She had grown up in Gary, Indiana, and was first heard singing along with the hits as she worked part-time in a record shop. She was signed by a Chicago company, Toddlin' Town Records and recorded her first single *Love Is Tears*. Later her claim to fame came from writing material for Stevie Wonder; in fact she participated on every Wonder album between 1972 and 1976. Artists such as Merry Clayton, Franki Valli, The Soul Gang and The Emotions recorded her songs. She also helped on albums by Roberta Flack, Minnie Ripperton and Weather Report. She had been in Stevie's backing outfit Wonderlove. He gave her so much advice and help and she's always been grateful. She felt he had so much talent that anyone working with him stood to gain.

Another music personality who took an especial interest in both her writing and vocal talent was Maurice White of Earth, Wind and Fire. He asked her if she would sign for his label and perform her own material. It was a thrilling offer and from it came the hit single *Free* and *This Is Niecey* which reached thirty-two in the UK charts. Her second album was to be entitled *Songbird*. She had a follow-up hit to *Free* with *That's What Friends Are* and *Baby Baby My Love's All For You,* an up-tempo number contrasting quite strongly with the sureness and slowness of *Free*. She enjoyed a bubbling disco smash with Johnny Mathis on the DJ tongue-title throwing credit *Too Much Too Little Too*

Late and reasonable success with another single *You're All I Need To Get By*. Then came chart silence until she suddenly soared into the singles listing when her catchy *Let's Hear It For The Boy* reached number two, kept from the valuable top spot by Wham's 45, *Wake Me Up Before You Go*.

She had become known for something more than an ability to gain good reviews, hit records and a history of working with big names. She had a growing faith. Deniece, had, like so many, rejected the church, and gone her own way believing that was the true way to freedom. Yet she never completely forgot her faith nor lost her belief that God was there. She often found herself thinking about it. She had a good friend in Philip Bailey and had taken part in his famous Jesus At The Roxy venue gathering (see Philip Bailey). But it was all part of what she has described as 'talking about Jesus time' rather than a time to make a commitment to Him and let Him take over. 'I hadn't allowed Christ to live in me,' she said at a later date.

Later she said more to me and to others, answering the time honoured question of the compatability of the music business and faith by saying it is a hard marriage unless there has been a definite response to Jesus. 'It's only difficult when your mind is not made up. Being around other Christians and being accountable to them is also important and surprisingly there are some great musicians who are Christians.' She had four in her secular music band.

She expressed further how the situation changes if you think of life and work as an offering to God, to honour His name. 'When you remember that Jesus is the star of your life and not you it kind of helps you to put things in better perspective – you are a servant.'

In the summer of 1985 she talked of a religious album she was recording for Gateway Music House. She had failed to persuade CBS-Columbia that they should release such a record. Martin Wroe in *Strait* commented on this to the effect that they probably feared a small sale in comparison with an ordinary secular release.

She is staying with the wider world of music and taking advantage of the fame that has been growing by leaps and bounds despite lack of success in the British charts between 1977 and 1984. Various awards have come her way and she has hosted some major musical events. The Japanese musical world gave her the Best Singer's Award for her song *Black Butterfly*, and she recorded a single for CBS-Columbia, *Living In A Video*, that has a definite Christian slant. She was one of the major names appearing at Greenbelt in the summer of 1985.

She returned to headline in August 1986. The release of her first total inspiration album, *So Glad to Know*, co-incided with her visit. She describes the album as an answer to a long-time prayer, saying 'I've tried to include an inspirational song on each of my past pop albums, but I've always wanted to devote an entire musical project to God. Now I have, there is a special song in my heart that can only be sung to Him.'

Deniece Williams provides a positive witness to the Gospel, not only to other black artists who have had a similar background but turned their back on their faith, but also to pop fans in general. She tells them that to be free you have to know Jesus. He gives real and lasting freedom.

Candi Staton

Several artists sang *Stand By Your Man* though it was Candi who triumphed in the US. Her version made little impact in Britain, but one single succeeded both sides of the Atlantic, *Young Hearts Run Free*. It was her first British chart appearance and just missed the top spot. Her only other British hit which almost made the top spot was *Nights On Broadway* though she had lesser success with three other singles *Destiny, Honest I Do Love You* and *Suspicious Minds*.

Even the excitement of hit records pales compared with one dramatic moment in her life. That was the time when she chose a totally new direction and with it a totally new approach to what she was aiming for in the music business. She expresses it simply. 'I used to sing a song called *Victim* ... I'm no longer a victim, but a victor. I used to sing a song called *Young Hearts Run Free* ... yet now I've found the only real freedom I've ever known in Jesus. I used to sing a song called *Stand By Your Man* ... now I stand by Him because He is the way, the truth, and the life.'

To become a Christian enabled her to break free but it was not without a struggle, an upheaval and a wrestling with her mind and conscience. She could say, 'I am a "new creature" in Christ Jesus ... and how I love it!!! I never knew how much joy there could be in the body of Christ. Praise be to our God, the Father, Amen!' Strong words which would have stunned some of those in her club audiences of the 1970s.

Gospel music had been a formative experience. Originally Candi, her sister and a friend had formed The Jewel Gospel Trio. 'We were like the Jackson Five. We could sing too and I tell you we floored them everywhere we went. We were bad. We were bad good . . . we were really good.' It was the famous Sam Cooke who thought she might sing the blues at a time when the blues were disparaged by most of those who listened to gospel and you did not sing both gospel and blues. They were considered incompatible, one representing the Lord, the other, man. 'You couldn't do it because they wouldn't accept you.'

Sam Cooke succeeded, and eventually Candi, like Aretha Franklin, turned to R&B with a degree of success. She learnt her craft in what were known as the 'smoky chitlin clubs' in the southern states that flanked the mighty Mississippi. It was all done with a degree of duplicity, for she was still a gospel and choir singer by day, but at night the gown and neatly slung hair were replaced by a low cut dress, hair arranged for effect and lyrics arranged to stimulate sexual desire. She found there was more to singing R&B than phrasing it in the same way as gospel and the audiences were certainly different. No one booed her in church or shouted sexual taunts. While in clubland almost anything was possible. She learnt new techniques of vocal artistry and ways of wooing an audience even if it meant flaunting herself.

Clarence Carter first persuaded her that she had a future in the music world. She recorded her first single at the famed Muscle Shoals recording complex with Rick Hall producing. The debut 45 title was the overlong credit *I'd Rather Be An Old Man's Sweetheart Than Be A Young Man's Fool*. Her eventual career had many ups and downs during the early period followed by a consistently successful period from 1976 to the end of 1978.

The success ended abruptly when *Honestly I Do Love You* left the charts at the end of June. It stayed only three weeks in the listing, hardly commensurate with the three-month run of *Young Hearts* in both Britain and America. For a period she threw in the towel. She solved her problems with management and record company by simply opting out and escaping back home to the family in Hansville. It seems that too many people were taking financial slices out of her life and draining her energy too.

In 1978 she was a mere support to the Stylistics when they toured Britain but had an interesting record release that year in the album *House Of Love* on which she sang both *Stand By Your Man* and the time honoured quasi-religious song *Take My Hand, Precious Lord*. In 1979 she released *Chance*.

She was now firmly in the pop trap of the time, where the singer was something well and truly subservient to the record company. There was a lull for some eighteen months until the release of *Suspicious Minds* a single that was a fairly creative remake of the old Presley hit of 1969.

She had a career outside the recording studio too. She was a special guest on the legendary Dick Clarke's *American Bandstand* in 1975 and co-starred with Lou Rawls on the popular US show, NBC's *Midnight Special* in 1978. In 1979 President Jimmy Carter invited her as his special guest of the Black Music Association Dinner on the White House lawn along with Andrae Crouch, Joe Williams and Chuck Berry. In Las Vegas she opened for Ray Charles at the Aladdin Theatre and starred at the Flamingo Ballroom. Along the way she had sung with virtually every great American black artist including Aretha, Diana Ross, The Commodores, Johnny Mathis, the late Donny Hathaway and Al Gree. Her record *Stand By Your Man* had been nominated for a Grammy Award and there was a nomination for her version of Presley's *In The Ghetto*. The great artist had sent his wishes and appreciation for her version.

Decibel raising was not part of her act, phrasing and timing were.

Gloria Gaynor

Wednesday mornings often find me writing copy for *The Manchester Evening News*. On one occasion in July 1986 it turned out to be a morning even more chaotic than usual.

A press release and handout had been sent to me about soul lady Gloria Gayor. I learnt she had signed to new British company Stylus, that she had a new single and an album was on its way. Nothing unusual in that news, it could fit umpteen artists. However, two lines in the press release hit me straight between the eyes. First was the comment that Gloria had recorded a gospel song entitled *Stubborn Love*. Then, 'the latter track is of particular importance to Gloria at a time when Christianity is playing an increasingly large part in her life.'

I immediately telephoned her British publicity officer Nicola Barlow to ask if Gloria happened to be in the UK. She was, and so began the unexpected interview of the morning.

I had interviewed Gloria many times, especially around her collection of big hit singles that have included *Never Can Say Goodbye, Reach Out I'll Be There, I Will Survice* and *I Am What I Am*. I had heard numerous albums such as *Glorious, I Kinda Like Me, Love Tracks* and *Experience Gloria Gaynor*. She has a mighty voice, a great sense of timing and rhythm. But this was a very different occasion for Gloria told me, 'These days I'm thanking the Lord with my voice. I've always known about Christianity. I mean I went to church as a kid and my brothers have been involved in the church. But you know in recent years I've been concerned about my attitudes. I had slipped away and I just felt I wanted to go to church.'

She went and she felt the call of God to commit herself in a way she had never known previously. 'I thought I was a Christian but you know I didn't know the love of God, the love of Jesus for me. I went to a Baptist Church and I saw someone being made a member and telling of his beliefs. That wasn't me. I was disturbed. I went back home and I read the Bible.

'I had turned to Isaiah 7:14 and there it is prophesied that the Messiah would come. I read more. And you know God was in my head. But I said it has to be more. There is my heart too. I said "yes, Lord, it's in my head" but there and then I said I love Jesus, I love God. I must act like it and I must not give Christ a bad name. I prayed. I felt I was led into the company of people who took me into the ways of the Lord.'

So Gloria found herself amongst Christians. So she learnt a new love. 'I've sung for years about love but not this kind.'

Wherever she travels she goes to church. While in Briain during the summer of '86 she 'got out my A to Z and found some marvellous Pentecostal churches, especially one on Jersey. They were so marvellous to me, so warm and so welcoming but I found this everywhere.'

Gloria is aware that show-biz offers all kind of temptations and has been somewhat uncertain about the direction of her musical career now. Certainly she would love to make a gospel album but she is not attempting to climb into an ivory tower.

'I think it is important that artists stand up and declare. There are pop stars who advocate drug taking, or if they don't say it then they indulge in a life style that suggests they do. I believe Christians in the entertainment world must be open and clear. They must say "we are of Christ" and you know they should develop the Christian style and stance. I do not think Christian music stars should exhibit what is called the "ego".'

Gloria believes there are too many 'wierdo's in the music world,' and she is determined to confound the likes of 'Prince, Michael Jackson, the lifestyle of *Dynasty* and *Dallas*' with Christian claims and teaching.

As I scribbled down what she was saying she seemed so radiant. Her life has changed. She sang *I Am What I Am* and now she is who she is because of Jesus. That's real soul.

MOR Contemporary

B. J. Thomas

British and American tastes coincide but countless artists enjoy most of their fame on one side of the Atlantic only. B.J. Thomas is an example.

Thomas' British chart history is confined to one record, a pleasant MOR number called *Raindrops Keep Falling On My Head* from the film *Butch Cassidy and The Sundance Kid*. While he enjoyed a chart-topper in his homeland with this song it aroused only mild interest in Britain where it just made the top 40, competing with versions by Sacha Distel and Bobby Gentry. In the States, Thomas amassed 14 top 40 hits between 1966 and 1977 with five top tenners amongst them and apart from the film song he had another number one with *(Hey Won't You Play) Another Somebody Done Somebody Wrong Song*. It must have sent many DJ's into a tizzy as they attempted their familiar fast rap with the title!

His appeal has been marketed toward the younger middle-age group, or even older although he no doubt had fans of all ages. His career has been shaped by his Christian faith since he decided that his life had to have this real focus.

His early childhood years were devoid of close family relationships although he admits he cannot pass all the responsibility on to his parents. 'They were teaching me with the tools they themselves had been given, but it didn't take me long to realise that there were more life situations with which I could not cope than those I could.'

His family roots lay amongst Texas farming folk but his parents lived in Hugo, Oklahoma, where he was born on August 7, 1942.

He was hitting the song trail from his early teens but he could scarcely have visualised that he would have sold over 32,000,000 records by the 1980s.

Two major influences in the formative years of his music were Hank Williams and, later, Jackie Wilson. Williams was an Alabama boy who emerged on record in 1946 as a singer and bandleader of the honky tonk school with a vocal appeal that reached beyond that music. Few C&W singers remained free from his influences and when he died of a drug overdose in the back of a car on New Year's Day 1953 music lost a great.

Wilson came out of the industrial world of Detroit, Michigan, and had been discovered by Johnny Otis at a talent show. He replaced Clyde McPhatter in Billy Ward's Dominoes and had taken off as a solo artist four years later in 1957 with a pacey, punchy affair called *Reet Petite*. His first million seller *Lonely Teardrops* in 1958 was less demonstrative but he had other wild numbers amongst other ballad hits with *Doggin' Around* and *Baby Work Out* more reflective of straight R&B and dance.

Wilson encouraged, Thomas in his singing and he joined a Houston-based band The Triumphs. They aped, not unexpectedly for a rock'n'roll outfit, the kid from Tupelo, Mississippi, Elvis Aaron Presley but Hank Williams determined the shape of their success. Thomas and friends saw the film of William's life and he dug the song *I'm So Lonesome I Could Cry*. The Triumphs recorded the song and Scepter Records found themselves with a million seller. However, the group split, the others going on to college but Thomas stayed around developing his own career with enormous Stateside success. He couldn't stop the hits coming.

He was confronted by the usual dangers. He took drugs and he was not amiss to the odd fight. He realized that drug taking led nowhere, but like so many others he thought he could cope and the habit would be temporary. He could escape for a while and make the better times seem longer and the bad times shorter. Almost too late he found out that it leads to a dead end. Later he related this period to his youthful insecurity.

'It's hard to handle success, even harder to handle failure. My drug problem really took a hold on me after the mid-1970s. I was separated from my wife and kids and my drug habit was costing me three thousand dollars a week. I got to the point where I was really closely brushing death with overdosing. Really, I had given up!'

However, a friend of his wife had become a Christian and B.J. was taken to hear an evangelist called Jim Reeves (but not related to the famous artist!). What he heard sounded real, and Christian teaching meant something for the first time in his life.

'I turned to Jesus Christ out of self-preservation. When I accepted Him, all of a sudden I had no drug urge and I was completely freed from the addiction. No one was really more surprised than me!'

He was asked by writer and broadcaster Paul Davis if everything had really been that dramatic. 'It really was! I bowed my head a drug addict and accepted Jesus Christ as my Saviour. I said, "Lord, I give you my drugs because I can't stop them!" When I raised up my head, well I'm like I am right now! . . . if you need a miracle the Lord meets you where you are. I needed one and he gave me one.' Thomas says his perspective on life changed, so did his values. His family was reconciled and his family life was restructured and rebuilt on true love.

He found his musical career had a new dimension as well. 'I made a decision to remain active in the secular music industry. I was aware of the mixed emotions this would cause, particularly amongst Christians. At one time, the emotions and opinions of those around me would have determined my reaction, but now the Lord teaches me how to respond rather than react. Knowing that I am in the centre of God's will, allows me the freedom to respond to what He asks me to do.' He believes that he gives answers, responses rather than preaching – he tells what has happened to him.

These days he is a member of the Mid-City Bible Church, located between Dallas and Fort Worth but spends 250 days a year on the road. 'When away from church I can sit down and open my Bible in the hotel room even if it's just for five minutes. . . . I always look forward to being back in church among fellow believers.'

He believes that a Christian song can top the charts. Perhaps he would like to be the artist responsible!

Debby Boone

There are both advantages and disadvantages to having a famous father or mother as Debby Boone knows full well. Dad is Pat Boone, one of the great figures of the fifties and early sixties both in the pop charts and in the cinema.

Debby is one of four daughters, and is married to Gabriel Ferrer. They have one child. Her sister Cherry was the first to marry, followed by Lindy who presented Pat and Shirley with their first grandson, Ryan. The youngest daughter is Laury.

Debby was the most rebellious of the four girls, the one usually caught breaking rules – smoking cigarettes or coming home late. 'I had to learn, over a long period of time how much my parents really loved me. Today, I really value the things they taught me.'

She grew up in a deeply religious household with Pat particularly known for his religious records and his religious record company, Lamb & Lion. His testimony has been shared many times and it exercised enormous influence over Debby.

As The Boones the sisters have recorded a number of gospel albums, with Debby usually taking the vocal lead. She has a wide vocal range and has become known as one of America's best ballad singers, but anyone who has heard an album like *Heavenly Love* knows she can also be as gutsy as the next person. *Because I Love Him* or her 1985 album, *Choose Life,* produced by Michael Omartian, further demonstrate her flexibility. The girls have had an

American Grammy Award with their album *First Class* on which Debby sang a sensitive solo, *You Took My Heart By Surprise*.

The sisters made their debut in 1970, when their father and the then little known Osmonds toured Japan. Pat had promised his daughters that if they could find a song for the show then they could visit the Orient with him. The opportunity was too good to miss and they came up with a version of *What The World Needs Now,* a song from the prolific pens of Bacharach and David. It was very well received and the girls were away musically and, in this case, geographically as well! Polish and confidence have been two of their most valuable attributes and their ability to vary repertoire and easily learn new material has been an added bonus.

Debby has become the best known and her chart-topper *You Light Up My Life* sold several million copies. Unfortunately its success hasn't been repeated but Debby has continually had work and this has given her the confidence to know that she could well come up with some major hits.

Her career, however, is secondary to her. Far more important is her living faith that she describes as a daily walk with the Lord. 'Each day can be better – I've learned that that is only possible, though, if each day you learn to give more and more of yourself to the Lord, and really let Him be your guide and Heavenly Father.'

These and other thoughts have been published in her autobiography *Debby Boone, So Far* (Thomas Nelson) in which she has also discussed the potential conflicts in moral values and responsibilities that come from being a Christian in show-business. She agrees there is enormous pressure and it is easy to lose sight of spiritual things. But Debby feels she hasn't been tempted to compromise her faith. She has been conscious of God's hand on her life.

'We are to glorify God in everything we do. I know that when I perform, people are watching me, watching my whole life to see if I really live what I say I believe in.'

Her career continues, so does her faith. The two interrelate. She rejoices that she knows her Saviour.

Maria Muldaur

A long time ago Maria Muldaur had a worldwide hit with *Midnight At The Oasis* selling several million copies. The lady has been far from dependent on that one record and her long list of albums has drawn a considerable audience. Quality music has been the name of her musical career. Albums like *Waitress In A Donut Shop, Sweet Harmony, Southern Winds,* a self-titled affair, *Sweet And Slow, Open Your Eyes* and *There Is Love* have not set the world alight but nor have they been failures. She draws an audience wherever she sings.

Maria Muldaur was born Maria Grazia Rosa Domenica d'Amato, a name hardly likely to succeed over the airways, not where fast speaking DJs are involved! She was born in Greenwich Village, New York. Blues and big band music provided her early musical fare. At school she formed a group called The Cameos with three other girls and they sang Everly Brothers harmonies. Later she formed The Cashmeres. The group was short-lived but the lady had musical ambitions.

Eventually she teamed with John Sebastian, Stefan Grossman (a superlative folk guitarist), Joshua Rifkin, Steve Katz and others to form the Even Dozen Jug Band. Not surprisingly during the US folk boom of the late 1960s and early 1970s there was still competition, but this was to be a bonus for Maria. Lead vocalist in another jug band outfit – the Jim Kweskin Jug Band – was Geoff Muldaur.

Maria fell in love with him and joined the Jim Kweskin Band. They married and eventually left the jug band to pursue a more-or-less joint career releasing two albums, *Pottery Pie* and *Sweet Potatoes*. Their style did not fit any commercial norms but was part a protest amongst artists against the overshadowing of creative integrity by financial considerations. Geoff was later involved with well-known US bluesman Paul Butterfied under the name Better Days. Maria became a solo recording artist after involvement with a number of musicians on the Steelyard Blues film soundtrack.

Love dwindled during the mid-1970s and the duo quarrelled and finally each went their own way. Maria was left with daughter Jenny and her music. That the latter would provide for them financially was clear from the response to her self-titled debut album that included the song *Midnight At The Oasis*. It gave her an income and led to tours and both radio and television work. It was obvious that she was not the sort of pop artist who charts sometimes only when the song could not possibly fail. Some people felt she was a musician's artist but she was more than that.

She did not have a teen following for her music and songs were in a more sophisticated mode, reflective rather than physical. The lack of response did leave her discouraged and after her 1976 album *Sweet Harmony*, she withdrew from the music scene.

In 1979 her teenage daughter Jenny was involved in a major car accident near their home. Things looked bleak. Jenny's head had gone through the windshield and there was a strong possibility of fatal damage or irreparable brain damage. She might be victim of a stroke. She might survive as little more than a cabbage. It was a tense time that demanded all Maria's resources.

She was helped in a rather unexpected way. Bob Dylan had announced his conversion to Christianity and had released *Slow Train Coming*. Maria was a fan of his and she listened to this album a number of times. Dylan's words kept echoing in her mind and became inseparable from her thoughts. Slowly and surely she realised that now was the time to be honest with herself and acknowledge that there might be something in all this Christianity! She recalls simply falling on her knees and in sheer desperation praying that her daughter might live. She prayed for personal forgiveness and was aware of how far she had slipped from His path but primarily Jenny was at the centre of her thoughts. Jenny survived and was well.

Maria started serious Bible study. She moved into Christian circles and attended the Pentecostal black church of her producer Patrick Henderson. She was gripped by a power she had not felt previously. The sermon was powerful, as if delivered for her alone. When the preacher invited people to come forward and make a response she came and 'received the baptism of the Holy Spirit' and found it 'overwhelming and powerful. Once that happens, you feel like you are "zapped" by the Holy Spirit. There's no way you can sit around after an experience like that and say "I wonder if there is a God?" or "Maybe there isn't a God?" You just know, you know?' She was very aware that she had truly been born again.

While some Christian singers have felt their ministry to be to their fellow Christians, Maria saw her ministry in wider terms. 'I don't want to just cloister myself and be surrounded by Christians, because we all have to go around and share what we know about the Lord to everyone.'

So she has continued to release albums on secular labels but she has recorded also for the major religious record company, Word. The religious album was *There Is A Love*. Some found it powerful material but other Christians felt it was rather abrasive.

Referring to her career in secular music she commented, 'Jesus didn't go and study the Torah and lock himself up in the Temple somewhere. He went to where people were – working in the fields or fishing – and He got the same flak from the organised church of His day that I've found myself.'

She told Martin Wroe of Britain's paper *Strait*, 'I sing about love but I make sure it's an uplifting sort of love-song. I sing some funny songs like about what man is doing to the environment and one of the subjects that I sprinkle liberally into my set is the subject of man's relationship to God ... by the time I sing *What about the Price?* at the end of the show, people are really moved because it's done in a way that's not condemning.'

Maria Muldaur remembers what it was like to be an unbeliever. She is determined the Christian presence which non-believers see in her will communicate the spirit of Jesus. Other Christian artists might have a different ministry but all have one thing in common; they believe Jesus is Lord.

Dana

An attractive softly spoken Irish girl opened the door for me. Her name was Rosemary Brown but on record and stage she was called Dana.

It was years ago that I went to her parent's house in Wembley, near the massive sports complex and conference centre. I was writing a feature for a magazine and was invited to her home. The article was about her music and her career but as we shared our religious views the inverview became a friendly chat in which we talked about our faith and the state of the various churches. She talked of growing up in a loving Roman Catholic home but how for a time in her life she had rejected all religious commitment. God had seemed irrelevant and faith of little value.

Later she was to say, 'For a year I lost my belief that there was a God, I remember thinking that it was all an escape. I thought God was like a big lump of putty. If we had any fears or doubts, we'd take a lump of this putty and push it in the cracks and then go on. Just like an escape route.'

Her faith was rekindled at a school retreat. The priest noticed her melancholy and she shared her unbelief. He told her, 'You know if what you say is true and if God is an escape then to be a Christian would be the easiest thing in the world. It would be an easy life. But in fact, to be a Christian is the hardest and most challenging life you could live!'

It made sense to Rosemary. Slowly her faith returned

and she experienced a growing maturity in her spiritual understanding.

When we spoke at her parents' home a series of unforeseeable events lay ahead that would both challenge her faith and change the course of her career.

She was a fresh-faced, attractive Irish girl with a soft voice and a lovely manner. At the age of eighteen she won the Eurovision Song Contest with a pretty pop song entitled *All Kinds Of Everything*. Its simplicity seemed well suited to the uncomplicated nature of the artist. She had a follow-up hit with *Who Put The Lights Out* but then there was nothing until a recording contract with a new record company, GTO, saw her collect four hits in the 1976-8 period. Two of the four *Please Tell Him That I Said Hello* and *It's Gonna Be A Cold Cold Christmas,* made the top ten, while *Fairytale* was only just failed to gain a place in the last ten.

Between hits she became involved in several Christian organizations that including the Festival Of Light and Festival Of Jesus during 1971-2. 'I felt at the time that Christ was a very big part of my life and that I had to make a statement about it.'

'As a young child I always had a tremendous awareness of the Lord. I remember times even as a seven or eight-year old, when I would cry at Good Friday celebrations. Although it was in Latin and I didn't understand a word of it, it would still make me cry.'

She spoke out in a manner that perhaps previously she could never have believed possible. There was a time when she was terrified to single herself out and be different and she was equally afraid of hurting anybody else's feelings. She was even a little worried whether she should do so many religious programmes, and certainly her agent, who was Jewish, was concerned that she might be typecast and that this would interfere with the kind of image they were building for her.

During the years between her second hit and *Please Tell Him That I Said Hello* she appeared in the film *A Flight Of Doves* and had countless TV shows including *They Sold A Million* which won the Knokke International Television Festival in Belgium, 1973. She had her own BBC series *A Day With Dana, Wake Up Sunday, What's It All About* and she sang weekly on the *Rolf On Saturday – Okay,* BBC TV series. Major nightspots welcomed her. She passed by the rock world and possibly many of her own generation but there was a great response from an older age-range.

It was a persistant voice loss that alerted her to danger. When playing Cinderella in panto in Wolverhampton, and later when she was on the stage of a club in Liverpool, she haemorrhaged in her throat. As a result she saw a specialist, and an operation was performed in September 1975. She carefully followed the medical advice on resting and use of the voice, and all seemed well. She completed a 1976 summer season and was in Manchester rehearsing for a television show when disaster struck once more. This time the specialist told her that there was a growth on one of her vocal chords. He said it was affecting the other chord and she should take further medical advice. Within hours she was in hospital.

For a while she thought it was a minor problem but she grew apprehensive when she became aware of a disproportionate interest in her condition. Then she was shown a newspaper cutting in which the surgeon was reported as saying there was only a fifty percent chance that she would regain her singing voice and it couldn't be guaranteed. It was then she realised the growth might have been malignant. It was no longer a question of whether she would sing again, rather whether she would retain any voice with which to communicate. Recovery was a slow process and when she first undertook a small amount of work she had a relapse, and was back to where her recovery had started, the slow process that would begin with whispering for a few minutes and no more.

Previously she had had undaunted faith that things would come right but now she was definitely discouraged and severely depressed. She recalls sitting in her parent's kitchen in North London. Her parents were out and she was alone and in despair. She prayed. And then she thought she would make a call to the specialist. Her action was so right for he had wanted to ring her, but had been hesitant, to suggest she consult a singing teacher and an expert in this kind of situation. She did so and has been grateful ever since.

Her illness made her realise that her work had crowded out most of her personal life and it had become the pivot around which everything else revolved. She knew this was not the right way for the future. At this time also she became a much more secure person who would not be concerned whether the people she met socially liked her or not.

Dana saw the hand of the Lord in all this and in the blossoming love of her life. She met a softly-spoken bearded Irishman, Damien Scallon, a hotel owner at whose premises she had performed. They became friends and over a period of time exchanged letters.

She remembers the day when she noticed a change in the tenor of his writing. His Christian faith had become more vibrant and real, and not just one of the several important aspects of his life. He had given up his hotel after it had suffered severe damage from five separate bombings. She noticed he had a tranquillity about him that she had not previously noted. Her throat problems had by now taken over her attention and for a while their relationship remained dormant. But she thought a great deal about the charismatic experience that Damien claimed. She learnt more from his brother Ken.

Ken was a priest. She remembers a rather sterile prayer time and he, sensing this, had suddenly told her 'I don't feel the Lord wants me to pray with you, I feel he wants me to talk to you.'

The world seemed to stop still. She was transfixed. They talked about a living faith and the charismatic experience. She knew she must make a new commitment, that her faith had to be personal, between herself and God, and she found a new peace and joy, a freedom she had hitherto not known.

One result of her new experience was the decision to record a religious album for Word. She also had an Irish number one with *Toto Tuus,* a song expressing her joy in the visit of the Pope to Ireland.

In terms of record hits and charts life has been relatively quiet. She reached 44 in 1979 with *Something's Cookin' In The Kitchen* and 66 in 1982 thanks to *I Feel Love Comin' On*.

Doubtless she will be back and delighting MOR music lovers. But even hits come second to her joy in the marriage to Damien that has given her a young child, and in the living faith that is independent of musical success.

Sheila Walsh

Drifting might have gone higher. It was a commercial and infectious record. Admittedly it had some familiar traits as if one had heard it before but couldn't place it. It was catchy, however; the sort of tune that you found yourself humming and whistling, and then buying.

For Sheila Walsh it was a disappointment. This was her first attempt in the general record charts in Britain. Of course she longed to see her disc climb higher each week and hopefully into the top 20. But for Sheila the long wait produced little joy and the record never pushed past the 60 mark. Cliff Richard supplied some vocals and some people thought that this would help but it didn't.

There were some good reviews, some even saying it would have been a hit without Cliff's contribution. Sheila was interviewed for London's major commercial radio station Capital Radio and made the sort of statement journalist's spend a morning thinking up; she said, 'I think if Miss Piggy did a duet with Cliff Richard it would be a hit.'

There were a number of factors that contributed to the lack of success. There had been a go-slow and a short strike at the record pressing and distribution plant, and this affected sales of all company products. An established artist with fans waiting for the next record, could have survived the delay between promotion of the record and release but Sheila was a new name.

The promotion itself could have been at fault. Using

biographical material supplied by Youth for Christ, meant that Sheila was promoted as a Christian singer. Her faith is central to her work but this was not a religious song and its merits were understated. The associations with a religious faith probably caused a certain reluctance amongst DJs, producers and reviewers who do not want to be associated with a cause or a message with which they are not sympathetic. The promotion did not inspire confidence in the record.

Cliff's contribution was cynically received. It was interpreted as a cunning ploy to get Sheila's career off to a better start. This criticism was unfair however for she clearly had talent and used it throughout the record.

'Some of the DJ's have told me since that they didn't play it because they felt I was just trying to climb on Cliff's back and preach the gospel. I felt that wasn't fair, you're supposed to judge the song not what the person believes.' One thing is sure. The record did not advance past the sixty mark although it was probably much better than a great number of the records above it.

For those hearing the record on a general record show the name of Sheila Walsh was largely an unknown one but in other circles, especially the Jesus Music world, her name was very familiar. She was a high selling artist in contemporary music circles of the Jesus Music scene. In 1985 she could claim the highest record sales on any British Christian label when she was signed with Word Records. In the United States she had been nominated for a Grammy. She was the first British artist to top gospel airplay and sales charts in America. She also presented two series of the popular British TV programme, *Rock Gospel*.

She has toured the world extensively sponsored by various Christian organizations. Her voice can match anyone's and she seeks success in the secular field but, underlying what she does, is the definite stamp of her faith. She wants to tell all and sundry the good news she personally knows and accepts.

Invariably she seems a contradiction to some people. Some cannot imagine a Christian singing anything but hymns and spiritual songs and there is a more obvious dichotomy in her own life. The US journal *Contemporary Christian Music* said 'She is a paradox. Although her stage persona is that of a reformed punk-rocker, she has rarely veered off the straight and narrow in all her years.'

Sheila's upbringing was in fairly strict Scottish Baptist circles. It was good Christian home. Jesus laid claim on her from an early age. Some of her schoolfriends thought she had a little too much religion! She studied classial voice and opera from her early teen years and grew to love the big soaring orchestra, the drama of opera, and the thrill of the voice battling against all and dominating. It gave her a strong sense of the dramatic and gave her assurance. Her Christian committment was made when she attended a gospel concert in Ayr's Odeon cinema. Soon she had ideas of being a gospel singer and she linked up with a local middle-of-the-road evangelistic band. Her classical teacher was not impressed, at least on a musical level. But the change also produced immediate problems for Sheila.

'I had to learn to untrain myself and sing from the head and throat and use this alien thing called a microphone!' Singing pop still causes slight problems for Sheila for her voice is often denied its true vocal range.

Being part of the group gave her a new perspective on her future. She began to see that God could make great use of the vocal talent with which she has been blessed. 'I began to see that God might want me to use my art as a means of communicating my faith to those who wouldn't come near a church.' She told Betty Wilson of *New Christian Music* that she felt this was as valid as being a missionary in far-away Tibet which was what she had previously considered.

Soon an important choice had to be made. She could go and study at the Royal Academy of Operatic Art or attend Bible College. She chose the latter. She believed this was God's will for her. Of her Bible College training at London Bible College she told Betty 'If that is where God wants you to be, it's the best place in the world. If it's your own bright idea you'll be miserable.' This is typical of Sheila's straightforward way of talking with journalists.

Her singing career really took off after a period spent with British Youth for Christ. During this time she gained enormous experience from meeting people face to face rather than from a stage and also learning to sing in the most varied of surroundings, where the acoustics differed sharply from one place to another and stage presentation could not be predicted.

She found herself, not unexpectedly, with a record contract from a religious record company. Her first album *Future Eyes* was launched in April 1981 at an annual Christian event called Spring Harvest, held in Prestatyn, North Wales. A single called *Here With Me* was taken from the album.

Gradually she became aware that the age range of her audience was changing from that she had known when working solely with Youth for Christ. This organisation was geared towards young people, as its name implies. Her audiences were correspondingly young. Sheila's increasing appearances at major Christian events saw a very much older gathering and many were not at all impressed by hearing the gospel coming across in MOR rock. Probably *It's No Secret* or a well-known gospel song would have been more acceptable. What is more, Sheila wanted to broaden her horizons, including the song lyrics in which the Gospel was seen to relate to all of life, a truth which is often understated.

Sheila had been conversant with preaching and singing for young people and she understood their problems such as peer pressure on issues such as drugs and promiscuity. She understood the lostness they experienced through searching for their answers in the punk culture.

'It's not that we're a generation of young people who know about God and have rejected Him. We've got generations that don't know what it is to be a Christian.'

For a while she conformed to the demands of people to whom she now sang but as she said, 'In some instances most of the audience were in their fifties and I was happy to fit in with that. But at the end of my concert I sold some 50 copies of my album, *Future Eyes,* which was nothing like the songs I had sung during the event. I felt guilty about it because it was not representative of everything I was doing.'

Her next album was softer and expressed the worshipful side of her overall Christian experience. However, she told Betty Wilson, 'I do want to carry on in the vein of *Future Eyes* because the Lord has given me a burden for a lot of young people who are struggling with self-acceptance and failure.' Sheila brought with her a specific youth ministry and a correspondingly snappy pop-oriented stage presentation. It was not simply a vivacious radiant girl buzzing with vitality backed by some musicians. There were constant visual explosions and indeed anyone unfamiliar with the current styles of music presentation might have wondered what was happening!

Sheila felt some qualms when she heard that a well known American figure from Sparrow Records would be arriving in Britain to meet her and attend some concerts. 'I was afraid of what he might think, because we use a lot of effects – lighting, fireworks and things. I thought he might have liked the album (*Future Eyes*), but he'd hate me in concert, but he really liked it!'

The album was remixed for the American market and Sheila found herself in the States discussing a major tour with artist Phil Keagy that would take in thirty-eight cities, starting from Austin, in Texas, and winding up in Boston, Massachusetts. A new chapter in her career was opening by God's grace and the problems of defining her audience and the kind of material she should record were no longer relevant. Her ministry could define itself in a contemporary mould without compromising with those aspects of the general pop scene that were incompatible with her faith.

She met a Christian guy by the name of Norman Miller who worked at Word Records and had been very much involved in bringing the Christian music world into the modern age. He joined her band and was a potent force in expanding the horizons of her career. Their engagement was announced at the 1981 Spring Harvest and together they have become a formidable partnership.

Sheila says she does not think about success. 'I tend just to give myself to whatever I'm doing at the time. Sometimes that means singing to 20,000 people at a festival or it may mean singing to just a hundred or so of my friends in a meeting... I know it sounds trite but ultimately the only success that counts is if we've done a job that is pleasing to God. That doesn't mean necessarily something flashy in worldly terms. It may be something we've done to the best of our ability trying to please Him.'

When asked by Paul Davis how important a hit single is to her she told him, 'Well, I'd say it's important in the way I see things. We tend to look at things humanly even though we still want God to direct. If I had a hit single it would enhance what we're doing. But I don't want to compromise along the line. I'm thrilled that my record company are keen on having a hit single and then doing TV. If I have a hit now – people know I'm a Christian. It's good they know from the beginning, so I don't need to spring that on the public at a later date.

The public attitude to her Christianity can be a strain. Whatever the pressure she maintains her stand. 'I can only say how in the end that I can continue because I know God accepts me as I am. I am aware of how inadequate I can be, how I can fail to reach what is supposed to be me. But His grace is so plentiful. I find that so marvellous. Yes, God accepts me. He doesn't expect me to be the greatest. I will make mistakes.

'Fortunately I belong to a great church. They don't issue dire warnings but if they don't agree with something I've done or might be doing they say "Look, Sheila you do this or that well but perhaps you might do . . ." and I feel their prayer support. They know people have been led to Christ through my work.

'It's great to have a small bunch of real friends. And someone like Cliff has been terrific. I've really benefitted from his advice. I've had some pretty awful letters and he's taught me to take these things calmly. You know I can get letters that make me so happy but there are some that say awful things and I've cried reading them.' There is not only the sure knowledge of God's grace, the treasure coming from a strong prayerful church, there is an awareness of God's call.

'I find that the most fantastic, you know being in the right place, learning to speak in contemporary culture. My television series on BBC brought tremendous mail. I had a letter from a seventeen year-old who had drug problems but thanks to watching *Rock Gospel* he suddenly realised he was wasting himself, his body, his life. He had decided he must find out more about this Jesus. Someone else was impelled to get the Bible out and read it for the first time in years and to make a response.' There are many more such stories. She is fond of quoting a letter that said simply, 'If only we'd known God was that exciting we'd have thought about Him more.'

Of *Rock Gospel* she says, 'The opportunities for talk are important but actually I think the music is just as important as the talking, after all it is a music show. Christians sometimes think that if they had opportunities like mine they'd put the Gospel across every week, but what they don't realise is that if they did, that would the be last series. My long term vision is of a gentle re-education in what Christianity is really like, but we have to keep on asking God to show us how to use our opportunities wisely.'

To a degree it was ideas such as these that caused some Christians to question the series and indeed to ask whether true Christianity was evidenced. They even doubted the conviction of some of the artists involved.

Sheila says, 'Jim [Jim Murray the producer] didn't want to alienate people who were not Christians by appearing "too preachy".' Some Christians felt it all too old-fashioned and conservative with predictable interviews. Some thought that the audience were always unduly enthusiastic, as if determined to show the world how happy Christians can be. Sheila accepted some of the criticism but pointed out that life is a learning process. Some criticism can cause unnecessary hurt especially that made in ignorance of the limitations imposed by the television medium. And Sheila says quite cheerily that there are some wallies in the Christian world, 'just because we are Christians doesn't mean we lose all our idiots!'

In an interview for the British radical evangelical religious paper, *Strait,* Martin Wroe suggested that *Rock Gospel* did not represent an infiltration of Christians *into* the media – rather it was simply the imposition on the media of a part of a religious music sub-culture. 'Instead of Sheila performing on *Top of the Pops* or *The Tube* we have Sheila presenting a whole array of Christian artists, ninety per cent of whom could get on neither of those programmes in their own right – they merit a T.V. slot by virtue of religious commitment. We ought to know by now that our (the Christian) calling is to offer the preservative and flavouring of salt to our society.'

Sheila was offered the series and as she replied to her critics, 'There's a lot of truth in what you're getting at but it's an opportunity we took; we didn't dream it up, the B.B.C. approached us.' At the same time she agreed damage can be done by 'trying to drop a bit of your Christian culture into the middle of the secular culture.' Martin concluded his article by remarking that a writer of Britain's most successful pop magazine *Smash Hits* wouldn't have a clue as to her identity but he also believed Sheila has no intention of restricting herself to a religious ghetto – 'she continues to be a superstar that few have heard of, chasing that elusive hit single' and that would indeed seem to be the case. Sheila Walsh comes across as a Christian and a musician who, like the faith itself, doesn't recognise the conventional religions and secular boundaries. She goes where she feels called and adds 'I'm trying more and more to see things from God's perspective.

'Also I do not think it's important to look and look at someone else's ministry and say they do it in a particular way and then to conclude it is the right way. I think we should feel happy that tremendous things happen through many ways of doing things. Some people will be used at certain kinds of gatherings, others elsewhere.'

Sheila's rapidly growing career and ministry often causes her to have a full diary which keeps her away for weeks, sometimes months, from her home in the small English village of Cobham. Such a full schedule can often mean that a person does not have enough time to stop and reassess the current position. Through all this activity she has realised just how important a sure faith is in her life.

When she does examine her life any sense of inadequacy is seen in a positive light.

'I feel God so often shows me how things are. As long as you're prepared to listen and be aware then I think things can happen. God allows me a close look at my own heart. I think people are surprised when I say I go through hard times. But I think going through them does bring me nearer people with problems.

'I think in the Kingdom way there is no time to say there is not a way to live now, tomorrow. Every now and then I say I must do some serious Bible study. I've been reading the Gospels and I've been so moved by the scandal of the Cross.

'There is an American singer called Michael Card who has an album titled *Known By The Scars* and it's a series of songs on the cross. It's very powerful stuff. I don't think I've ever believed in the Bible so much as I do now. You know to do things our way is disaster, to do them His way is to find the sure path.'

A second series of *Rock Gospel* was successful and in 1986 she released a new album, *Shadowlands*. Sadly a big British tour had to be cut short because of voice and throat problems. Perhaps significantly her autobiography was published called *God Put a Fighter In Me*.

Back to her song *Drifting*. She is doing precisely the opposite with her life. Whatever happens in her career she stays true to the real meaning of the Gospel. That is not drifting!

Classic Pop-Rock People

Barry McGuire

Barry McGuire sent shivers of fear and apprehension through the kids in the mid-1960s. He sang *Eve of Destruction*. It was a world hit and has become a pop classic. No singer since has repeated his success with that song.

McGuire sang of imminent destruction to the world. He talked of the hate that existed in the world of the early Sixties; there was US confrontation with Red China, Russia and North Korea. The super-powers tested nuclear bombs and polluted the atmosphere. There were a number of potential clashes that could have caused nuclear devastation. For McGuire there was another battle taking place, a personal one. The kind of life he was leading threatened his own Eve of Destruction.

McGuire had been a member of the New Christy Minstrels, a successful US folk act that owed not a little to McGuire's throaty vocals and his overall energetic drive. In America they hit the top 40 three times thanks to *Green, Green, Saturday Night* and finally *Today*. The hits came in 1963, two years before Dylan hit the singles scene with *Subterranean Homesick Blues* and a year before the Beatles' invasion of America.

McGuire despaired of the New Christy Minstrels. They were too soft, safe and hardly in tune with the coming social and political furore that was to charge through the teen world and rock music.

He told me, 'It was the time of the Byrds and *Tambourine Man*. Bobby was around (Dylan). I guess I had made thousands of dollars and I went through the star trip thing. It was fun for a time but it's like riding a roller coaster, fun for the first four or five times but a big drag when you get past thirty. Even at this time the drug thing was coming my way. Two of us in the group would get up in the morning and roll 15 or 20 joints, enough till we crashed that night.

'On vacation I met Phil (P.F.) Sloan. I really liked the guy. You know I've always had words and tunes going round in my head but I can't capture it on paper or in the studio. This guy was into writing music and had had four or five hits with people like The Turtles and Johnny Rivers. Phil had this song *Eve of Destruction* and I dug it. We said to Lou Adler, who was working with him, we'd make the disc. We had intentions of it being the B-side, we didn't think anyone would play it, too heavy.

'Everyone comes along and said it was a pseud but man, I did believe in it. I couldn't stop people making it a jukebox hit, a dance hall blast. At this time in America there was this incredible violence, you had the black and white problem, there was lying from so-called responsible bodies – I mean government leaders, churches – there was this generational thing.

'I was looking for truth and what I saw, I saw with Phil, things were coming into chaos rhythms and I believe we had to have a change.'

McGuire had grown up in sunny California, the son of a construction worker. The young McGuire had dreams of joining the navy and managed to enlist by lying about his age.

He was found out and he found himself working among the fishing people in San Pedor, California. He was around 19 when he quit to work as a pipe fitter in the construction industry. He stuck around there until he was 25. As for music, like many other people, he sang for friends, in his case when everyone sat outside during the hot sultry summer evenings. He sang at a friend's birthday party and was heard by someone who owned a nightclub. He was offered a week's spot, accepted the offer, invited his friends and did well out of tips. At first he found it hard to accept that people paid him money to sing but a spate of club bookings led him to think of music as a career. Within twelve months his vocals fronted the New Christy Minstrels.

Money flowed in. He was a celebrity. He recalls, 'People, cab drivers, would say "Hey, didn't I see you on TV last night?"'

It was fun because it was new ...

He became caught up in the dubious life that surrounded many singers – drugs. He also had more serious questions on his mind and to suppress these he moved into reds and amphetamines.

'I started experimenting with different effects and what it did to my performance on stage. I pretty well lost contact with people because of the one-nighter thing. For four years it seemed like a dream. From one place to another, to another, to another! There was nothing real! It was just a big fantasy.'

One person who tuned into his wavelength was a friend called Paul. The two read and re-read books on neurology, astronomy, biology and psychology. 'We wanted to find out what we were all about. We would lie there stoned and just read and read and read. Paul would tell me all the time that he was terrorized and filled with fear.

'He looked the most calm of persons but on the inside he said he was just eating himself up. We finally reached a point where we wouldn't perform any more because our show was such a lie.'

Barry's first acid trip was in 1965. Paul had gone to San Francisco. He phoned Barry one day and told him to stay put because he was on his way with something special. Paul came in with the acid, very much the 'in' drug. The trip was a good one for Barry felt doors were opening.

'I thought psychedelics were the key to open the door to inner reality and inner truth.' The stoned singer made it big with *Eve of Destruction* and there was money to further the drug taking and the quest. This was the beginning of acid therapy.

'I went down with three other guys to Mexico. First we went to Port Varde and when we didn't dig that, it was moving down to Zuwateneo. That was far out and I had my heaviest trip. I got this picture of all of us being gods and when I returned to the States I was searching for a guru and I wanted to free people from their bondage of morality.

'I was tired of being a plastic cabbage, a pop star and I thought to be totally free was to be bisexual. I thought homosexuals were just as repressed as heterosexuals and to be free was to make it with everything – a tree, animal, a person. What was the difference, for you were a liberated human god.'

Barry met the famed Timothy Leary in Mexico. Leary was the high priest of drug taking.

'To me LSD was the breakthrough into spiritual awareness, that's why I got into it. I don't remember having any really bad trips though there were some unpleasant tones. Drugs make you aware and if you see the human race on a bad trip then you become much more conscious of this poverty. You see the human race rolling toward destruction and it's more painful than reality.

'Suicide did occur to me but I didn't want to lay my death on the people I loved. I didn't want them to receive the news. I was destroying and was destroyed and my body was dead. My drug kick was from '62 to '71. I still sang. I always feel like singing.'

As the man once said to me 'I ain't lived a pure life, and you've heard some of the story.'

McGuire's life continued in this pattern for a number of years, until the time he appeared in the Broadway production of the musical *Hair*.

'I really felt that *Hair* was a statement of liberation to break down the barriers between male and female, black and white, rich and poor, old and young... We were spiritual beings living in the realm of material things, and we had to get over all these hang-ups.'

McGuire found *Hair* another lie. While on the surface it expressed the late Sixties philosophy and fitted in with the cries that echoed around the Woodstock rock festival of 1969 'peace, love and freedom', beneath the top layer the money- machine was well-oiled.

'It was just another Broadway rip-off. It was like someone just came along and exploited the Hippie philosophy. Everybody wanted to believe in it but everybody wound up just getting ripped off. Then the street-people wound up just leaving the show because the professional actors would just slice them right out because they were in the show for their careers and the street-people were in the show for spiritual reasons ... they were trying to get a message across to humanity.'

So Barry moved to Hollywood and with a buddy called Denny it was back to lots of drink and drugs. It was like old times again.

'We would take anything that would come into the house. In fact, we would say "Don't tell us what it is, we want to be surprised!" We wouldn't know if we were going up, down, in, out, sideways... Then, I really fell into a relationship where I discovered within myself all of the jealousy, greed, and the animal hatred that I thought had been eliminated from my life.'

McGuire was promised a 'new day' but received only a

re-adaptation of an old one. However, his life was about to be changed and the instrument of change was unexpected.

McGuire was just going along a street one day minding his own business, when he was confronted by a stranger who was out telling people about Jesus. In spite of all his spiritual searching McGuire had never encountered the Christian faith.

The street evangelist was telling people that Jesus loved them and He would be returning to the world soon. McGuire paid attention. He went away and began finding out about Christianity. He took his time and researched carefully, as had been his wont in the past when he and buddies had explored all kinds of philosophies. Twelve months passed and Barry felt he could accept the claims of Christ for himself.

'I kept becoming more and more aware of his presence in my life and in the reality of the world. I got hold of a New Testament and read that. It really blew my mind! I *knew* that Jesus had come and been crucified for *our* sins.'

McGuire felt he had to respond to God's mercy in sending His Son and that through His Son the price of sin had been paid. 'I had to deal with that. I didn't want to. I tried to just shine on the whole thing. I figured, well, I have just made the wrong choice and there is no way I can ever come back into a relationship with God because my life was so foul and filthy and evil.'

McGuire went crazy on drugs, girls and booze. He took part in a film on the satanic Hell's Angels motor-cycle gang about devil worship. It was called *Werewolves On Wheels*. 'It blew my mind . . . I was really playing into the hands of Satan. I was really being used by Satan to glorify his kingdom of darkness, sexual violence, drugs, tarot cards and the occult. It blew my mind! But I thought, "Wow, that's the way it's gotta be!" I made the movie while I was running from God and it just seemed like I was making the last effort or something.'

McGuire felt there was an assurance in his acting that he had never attained previously. 'It's like Satan was really offering me the world in return for my soul because as soon as I finished that film I had another film offered to me. It was really incredible!' McGuire couldn't keep on at this pace. He would either crack up completely or he would have to find some kind of peace.

Not surprisingly the turn-about was sudden. He was confronted again with the Gospel claims and suddenly it happened.

'It was really far out! I had the total realisation that I was lost, not *only* me, but all my friends! The whole human race was lost!

'I just thought, man, there is no sense in this. I've done everything there is to do. I was lying on the floor moaning, "What am I going to do?" A friend of mine came over and asked if something was wrong. I said, "Yeah man, WE ARE!" ' McGuire had reached the age of 36 and it was only then he realised there was 'no sense to him at all.' He called into play analogies of the amusement park and fairground.

'It was like when you go to an amusement park and you want to ride all the rides. So, you go on all the rides. Then you remember the *best* rides. Some of them are good and some of them are *really* good. So, you want to go on the best rides all over again. So, you go on the best ones again, and then you go on them again, and again! Pretty soon you say, "It's no sense in going in this amusement park again. It's time to leave!" That's what I felt about my life. My life was like the amusement park and I had gone on all the rides!

'The ones I dug I had gone on a couple of times until they lost their thrill. There were just no more rides left! Even the best rides in the park didn't make it for me any more! So I thought, I may as well just check out! This is a big drag.

'Suicide was my thing right then. I had to decide whether I was going to go out and kill myself or whether I was going to give my life to God!'

McGuire threw himself into the hands of God. He felt God was saying to him 'Man, if you give your life to Me, I will heal it! I will make you a brand new person!' 'I didn't think that could ever happen because of the snake-pit in my life. I said, OK, if you want me, you have got yourself a boy! I gave my life to Him that night!'

The venue was a Hollywood party!

The immediate effects of this dramatic happening were that McGuire turned away from drugs and he stopped having sex with girls who were hanging around. He soon returned to his old ways, however, but at least this time there was a capacity to fight back and McGuire saw plainly what was happening. He spurned an old girl friend who had turned up with a bag of new dope that was as yet untried. He left Hollywood and went to his uncle who lived in Fresno. His uncle was a Christian and invited Barry to attend church with him. It hardly excited Barry since conventional churches turned him off but he went. The church was hot and sticky and the visiting preacher was uninspiring. 'He might as well have been reading the grocery list. I really got bummed-out!' McGuire wondered what he was doing there. He had seen all this before. It was the very atmosphere that had turned him off.

But his reaction was a trifle premature. Some young people began to tell of the change in their lives. Suddenly the atmosphere had altered. He knew there was something different and true in their lives. They gave simple and uncomplicated testimonies of how Jesus had changed their lives, healed them, and set them free; given them a love, and a power and a reality.

'I knew what they were saying was true. You know

when you hear something like that and they are living the truth that they are telling – that's power! The power of God was there! After the service we went outside and they prayed for me. That's when I really felt the spirit of God. He came into me that night, and really gave me the power to overcome my flesh, to die to my flesh, and to be born-again a new creature. Since that time it has been a steadily, growing and learning experience. How to walk in the Spirit; how to walk in faith; learning how to trust God in everything; and to know that God is going to come through.'

McGuire entered another long period of soul-searching introspection, and spent hours with the Bible as he sought to find out who God was. He had a million questions that needed answering. 'It takes time to get into the Word and to grow in faith.'

He found a vibrant bunch of young Christians who allowed him to be himself. He said of them, 'They really gave me the love of God in a personal relationship and really got me down into studying and prayer. They just grounded me in the Lord'. He read twenty chapters a day! 'You do that every day and that puts you through the New Testament every two weeks! You do that for three months and you find out a lot of things!'

The reality of the Gospel to Barry was simple. Too many things in his life had become false gods and they had come between him and God. 'Things that Jesus said put a whole new direction, a new thing in my life!'

What about Barry's old friends? Didn't they think he had just freaked out on something cheaper than drugs? They did, but they were sympathetic. Barry was happy, which was fine. However, they expected it to be short-lived, as brief as their own swopping and changing with drug use and abuse. Whenever he saw them they would ask if he was still with Jesus and when he replied in the affirmative they grunted the phrase of the time 'far-out' and left it at that. It saddened Barry. 'A guy who is into drugs (and really thinks he is where it's at) is just on a one-way street through the graveyard. It is really difficult to talk with someone who doesn't realise he has a *need*'.

He said he could only point out to people what he knew personally – the disastrous end caused by drugs of a number of pop stars including Jimi Hendrix, Janis Joplin, Brian Jones and Lenny Bruce.

He remarked how some people he knew had a brave exterior but are 'really lonely and unfilled but to get a person to admit that is almost impossible! The only thing I can do is just plant the seed that Jesus loves them, that He died to save them, and that if they ever come to the end of the rope they should simply reach out to Jesus and let Him heal their broken life.'

On US college campuses Barry got a better response. He was remembered as the guy of *Eve of Destruction* and people were genuinely interested in his commitment. Some expected him as the guy of old and initially were negative but once under his magic they listened.

New songs abounded in Barry's mind.

'I started receiving new songs of life and love that dealt with all the old questions I'd raised in *Eve of Destruction*. Although the new songs often reflect the despair and desolation of my yesterdays, they're always pointing to the healing that's available today and to the hope and promise of tomorrow.'

Barry signed with a major US religious recording company and an album entitled *Seeds* was issued in 1973. It remains one of his most powerful record statements. Soon there was another, *Lighten Up,* and along with the very talented Second Chapter of Acts a live set *To The Bride*. Sparrow signed him in 1976 and albums came thick and fast.

McGuire began spending more time heading the bill in Christian concerts and found himself a perennial favourite in Christian music circles. In 1980 he told the American magazine *Contemporary Music* that he was taking in 150 concerts a year, plus television shows, recordings and ministries. He spent some three or four months out of every year in Britain. But all the work took its toll.

'I get up in the morning and there's thirty-two things I do and I pump and pump and pump and by the time I get to the 25th thing I'm finished and I fall down and go to sleep.' He found his desk bulging with invitations, often in the region of 400 letters believing he should do this or that. 'It gets crazy! I keep pruning back the bush and before I know it I look and I've got a jungle growing out of my brains. I've got weeds growing out of ears and man I can't think. And I say STOP! Take all the phones off! And while the phones are off somebody knocks on the door!'

McGuire, confronted with ever-increasing demands, saw another message being spoken to him by God. He believed he was summoned to join The Agape Force and in 1980 he and his wife Mari resolved to spend five years on the staff.

Contemporary Music asked McGuire what was the difference he now saw between secular and Christian music. McGuire saw things in black and white.

'It's (music) either going to worship holiness, a relationship with God, thanksgiving, rightness, light; or it's going to worship emptiness, death, suicide, loneliness, violence, immorality.'

He talked of past times.

'Before I was a Christian the songs I sang were all songs that glorified death, or they glorified the insanity of drug immorality. When I became a Christian my songs started to reflect my relationship with life, understanding of life, understanding of creation, of His love, of His plan. A song by any artist is going to reflect the spiritual condition of that person.' He said music was just a form of expressing his emotional involvement, his involvement with the Lord.

'I listened to Bobby Dylan's album. I don't think there is anybody in this world that's got a worse voice than Bobby Dylan. There's nothing attractive – at least not to me – maybe some people think he's got a great voice – but I've never, since he was a little skinny kid in the Village, thought he could handle his voice.

'But the thing that captures me is his *involvement* with what he's doing. When he sings, he sings from the very inner-most part of his being – so it doesn't matter what he sounds like. It doesn't matter! You don't have to have a great voice to be a great communicator or a great singer. All you've got to be is *honest*. Bobby's always been honest – even when he was lost he was honest through lostness.'

McGuire said he wanted to make music that is so true that everybody would be able to identify with it. People would say 'hey that's the truth' whether they are Christian or not. He reckoned he would be singing and playing at 105 God willing. For Barry at least, the eve of destruction is over.

Noel Paul Stookey

Noel Paul Stookey is a member of the world-famed Peter, Paul and Mary. These days they're hardly taking the pop scene apart but their re-forming after a lengthy period apart was greeted with pleasure by thousands. Their concerts attract full-house notices without the need for extensive promotion.

Back in the 1960s and early seventies they were amongst the best known names in the musical world. They were more successful in the USA than in Britian but popular in the UK nevertheless. Arguably, it was their hit with Dylan's *Blowin' In The Wind* in 1963 that contributed enormously to this. In their press interviews they extolled Bobby's songwriting and unusual singing technique. The public rushed to the record stores to buy Dylan's debut album *Bob Dylan* and then *The Freewheelin' Bob Dylan*. But Dylan had an abrasive quality that PP&M did not in spite of their own anti-war sentiments. Nothing in the Peter, Paul and Mary catalogue could rival the potential horrors of World War III as espoused in chilling fashion by Dylan through songs like *Talking World War Three Blues*, *Hard Rain's A Gonna Fall*, and *Corrina, Corrina* and *Masters Of War*. Much of their material has a folky edge that more resembles Dylan's debut album. Fans of the songs could choose which sort of delivery they preferred.

The trio were very much to the forefront of the early peace rallies and conventions at which the major folk artists of the time sang. They may not have had the sharp lyrics or vivid tongue of a Dylan or Phil Ochs but they certainly made people listen.

They had tremendous commercial success Stateside although some folk purists said they had defiled the style to achieve it. Folk purists did not pick up on the new electronic music sounds that were on their way. The music scene changed drastically once the Beatles hit America in 1964 and even more so in the folk scene when Dylan first used an electric guitar and became a major figure in rock music rather than solely folk-rock realms.

Peter, Paul & Mary led the way to general acceptance for a whole host of angry American singers. In those days fans were not accustomed to seeing message songs hit the charts. In the States, the same changes occurred but on a much larger scale, led by Dylan. Lilian Roxon in her definitive work on American rock, made very direct comments. 'When Bob Dylan happened in a small way, Peter, Paul and Mary, not thoroughly established, were able to make him happen in a big way by making *Blowin' In The Wind* one of the top ten songs of the nation.'

Lilian Roxon described their music as predictable, smooth and professional in formula and she stressed 'generally people at the top of the charts had previously stayed out of politics. Peter, Paul and Mary sang at rallies and marches, in the good old folk tradition, but with the additional advantage of a huge public following. They did have a hammer, they had a bell, they had a song to sing, and they sang where it counted.'

The trio had twelve US top 10 hits during the 1960s. The first of these was *Lemon Tree*, and others included *Puff The Magic Dragon; Blowin' In The Wind,* their fourth success in America, a little over a year after *Lemon Tree* and *Don't Think Twice It's Alright,* another Dylan composition. *I Dig Rock And Roll Music* followed and oddly enough they ended their chart career with a number one in the dreamy romantic strains of *Leaving On A Jet Plane*.

In Britain only four songs charted. These were *Blowin' In The Wind* in October 1963, *Tell It On The Mountain* and, at the start of the seventies, that American chart-topper *Leavin' On A Jet Plane* which was only kept out of the top spot by the relatively ordinary *Love Grows* from Edison Lighthouse. During January the group was unable to recover from a slowly falling chart place.

As a live act they could be magic. I watched them from only a few feet away when I stood in the wings of the DAR hall, Washington D.C. in 1969. They were more aggressive than their critics allow and could be quite raunchy although subsequently remembered mostly for slower material or folk songs such as *If I Had A Hammer*.

They sang of their concern for humanity from a general humanistic standpoint and there was little sign of any religious faith in their material.

However, at this time Noel was already asking questions about religion. A young man called Steve Hands had gone backstage while the trio were playing in Austin, Texas, and had witnessed to the power of Jesus in a person's life. Stookey was impressed; enough to pursue his quest with even greater energy. He was attracted by two diverse religious sources. One was the Bible, the other the Tibetan Book of the Dead. He had even talked with Dylan who suggested he should take long walks and he should read the Bible!

Stookey had begun searching for the most common reason of show-biz personalities and stars, he had grown dissatisfied with his opulence. He saw that much of the world he moved in was transitory and shallow. Certainly there was little, if any, sense of the spiritual. He despaired of champagne breakfasts, limousines, extravagance and waste. He also disliked the constant travel and separation from his wife and family. He knew he was to some degree living a lie and there was no inner peace. He believed there must be absolute truth that could be found, something which would shape him as a person, even recapture and revitalise the part of him which he felt had been lost amidst the frenetic world of stardom and its demands.

Finally he made his decision and became a Christian. It had momentous impact. He said 'My old life was discarded – I woke up the next morning and I was new – and the Spirit made me different. The old Noel was replaced by the new.'

Of course he had to share this experience with the others and the question inevitably arose as to what he should do in the future. Any decision would affect the future of the other two members very much.

He told people, 'I had comments from Mary that she felt responsible for defending Christianity because in peoples' minds she was somehow included through me. Mary also felt sorry for me. Peter, however, began to suspect that such a thing was inevitable for him as well.'

For Noel's wife, Betty, the decision was catastrophic. 'Betty was dismayed because it was like a parachute drop – the experience just came out of nowhere. My conversion was upsetting to her. The old Noel was replaced with the new.'

His conversion, together with an increasing desire to be at home and see things through, and the upheaval that his new found faith caused, led him to the decision to quit live work. He was already tired from a decade of show-biz pressure and travel. He also decided he wanted to be released from recording since even if the group stopped, the recording would continue to be a time-consuming business.

'But both Peter and Mary were concerned about performances and felt that just releasing records was not enough for them.'

Noel Paul reckons they thought this way because the group identity figured so heavily in their lives while for him now the 'group was something to participate in, but not the sum total.'

However, in 1970, when they were at their most popular, the group announced the end of the trio. Naturally there was great sadness amongst fans and a flood of letters asking them to reconsider the move. Later the trio would re-form but for now there were other priorities. Noel Paul spent an increasing amount of time with the family, which was what he had wanted. The Stookeys felt drawn to a more rural existence as an expression of their faith. They felt a return to basic values was necessary and resolved to leave the suburbs and draw closer to creation and God.

'The scales fell away from my eyes and I saw a great disparity between the man who grew tomatoes and me eating them. A disparity between those things made by man and those things made by God – and how much better it is to live near God.'

The corollary of this was the hunt for the right place, somewhere that could meet their new spiritual and material needs. They found it in Blue Hill, a rural coastal Maine community, after first finding a place in New Hampshire which became no more than a stepping-stone and was sold without much sorrow.

Maine became much more than a living home. They had an abandoned four-storey hen-house transformed into a recording and animation studio complex that went under the name of Neworld Media. Paul had continued recording with Warners during the demise of PP&M and the period when he was househunting and in 1971 had released *Paul And*. A single released from the album entitled *Wedding Song (There Is Love)* made 24 in the US charts and spent nine weeks in the top 40. However, there was no top 40 follow-up.

In 1972 his old friend from PP&M, Peter Yarrow, released a fascinating album for Warners entitled *Peter*. It contained a number of religiously inclined numbers including *Beautiful City, River of Jordan* and the superbly crafted *Greenwood,* with its derivation the words found in Luke 23:26-32 – sad, poignant, pithy words of Jesus – 'Daughters of Jerusalem, do not weep for me, but weep for yourselves and your children. For behold, days are coming in which men will say "Blessed are the barren and the wombs that never bore, and breasts that never nursed." Then they will say to the mountains, "Fall on us!" and to the hills "Cover us!" For if they do these things in the green wood, what will happen in the dry?' The track is one of the most moving cuts found in album history.

In the 1970s Noel produced a number of albums and they reflected his true inner peace. While he operated his recording studio his wife ran a commercial greenhouse across the road. There was a separate family garden and berry patch which was tended by all the Stookeys. Noel rarely listened to the Top 40 and instead preferred classical music. Bach was a particular favourite. Naturally there was some looking back. 'Those days with the group were provoking and challenging. I learned tenacity and a sense of thoroughness from Peter and from Mary.'

The possibility of PP&M re-forming arose in 1976. At that time Paul felt ambivalent and eventually intimated that it was not the right time. Two years later in June 1978 the reunion was on. He told *Contemporary Christian Music,* 'I would say that we are more compatible, that a certain amount of age and wisdom and distance has given us a surety, a kindness towards each other and an ability to be encouraging that we did not have previously when we were younger and growing and scrapping – and loving, but in an awkward kind of way. The voices are probably the most traditional part of what we're doing on the new record – the fact that you can hear the voices, you can identify them – and yet they produce a blend that is very unique.'

The come-back album was accompanied by tours including a visit to Britain in the 1980s. How did Noel square the return to the popular fray with his faith, now a decade old? He told *CCM,* 'I feel that, if God is the Truth then all we really have to assign ourselves is to be able to work in His service. The inverse is like walking through a forest of grass and saying 'meadow!'. Therefore as long as we address ourselves to the revelation of God's Spirit in the world – it seems to be a precarious line to walk because you must continually address Him to make sure that you are in His Spirit – when pressed on where you get your inspiration, it should be second nature to give God the glory.'

Noel Paul expressed how he felt his actions (and anyone's) would be judged by the world to be a reflection of 'what we believe in our hearts, we are judged on many levels – not only on what we sing and say, but the manner in which we sing and say it, and perhaps even how we dress when we sing it.'

So by the 1980s Paul Stookey had come full circle, but with a difference. He had spent a decade travelling in the presence of his Master. Now he sang as someone known as a born-again believer. He was not searching anxiously, but had found what he wanted and after a decade was still content with the decision he had made all those years ago. Over the years he had recorded several religious albums that had received high praise, including *Reel To Reel, Something New And Fresh* and *Band And Bodyworks.* Some considered the latter his strongest, and this was certainly true of the lyrics, and perhaps of the overall crafting. His composition *I Wanna Testify* had a rock feel and fire that the title deserved. The album had variety and was a most worthy testimony to this committed Christian.

Noel Paul Stookey's influence has been greater by far in his home country but such is the international popularity of the trio that it has doubtless touched lives beyond the US. While Christians may rejoice in his testimony and musical ability non-believers have been able to hear a message that might otherwise have passed them by.

Stookey's life remains full of promise. So many good things have happened for him. He still believes from his Christian base that the future is in God's hands and that it will be directed accordingly. He feels his work in life is unfinished. Thousands will profit from his future creativity. You are asked to walk like he does in the Lord's way.

Johnny Cash

They say that Johnny Cash destroyed so many hotel rooms that some motel and hotel owners refused to rent him rooms for the night. It reached a peak in 1967 when Cash was on the downward trail, physically, emotionally and spiritually. It was in total contrast to the life Cash knew when he was a kid. He was twelve when he made his decision for Jesus in a church in Dyess, Arkansas where he grew up in a strong Christian home. The commitment lasted into early manhood. It was to wither, almost die and then he flooded with new life as, at the age of thirty-nine, Cash walked to the front again at the Evangelical Temple in Nashville.

Cash was one of country-music's greats but such was the appeal of his gravelly voice and impressive charismatic stature that he attracted an audience far beyond the boundaries of country genre. In America he had definite appeal to youth in the 1960s. In Britain he had the occasional hit record. There are twelve hit singles listed for Cash in Whitburn's momentous catalogue *Billboards Book of Hits*. In Britain, the corresponding Guinness volume has five titles – *It Ain't Me Babe, A Boy Named Sue, What Is Truth, A Thing Called Love* and the last one in 1976, *One Piece At A Time*. But Cash is predominantly an album artist with no less than sixteen listed in the Guinness album book of British charting long-players. From these albums have come songs forever associated with Cash including *I Walk The Line, Folsom Prison Blues, Ballad Of A Teenage Queen,*

Ring Of Fire.

I remember the first time I met Johnny Cash. He was as I pictured him, from hearing the voice, reading about his career and knowing something of his personal life. He was tall, towering, strong in physique, with a face both tough and tender, lined with life's experience. He had presence, a no-nonsense approach that suggested his time had better not be wasted. As a reporter and a Christian I wanted to meet the legendary figure who shared my faith. But I was there to do a job, for Cash was sufficiently regarded to find himself in any encyclopedia of rock. In the *NME Encyclopedia of Rock* Cash is described as 'an individual stylist, his appeal reaches a wide audience. Own compositions reflect many traditional facets of American life, his simple, direct style varying little over the years.'

Elsewhere it's been noted that Cash is a man of many sides. In a large-scale pictorial story of his life part of the series titled *Country Music* (number 72 in the series) the writer notes 'there's the Cash who sings to convicts with the compassion of a soul brother who says "I'm one with you, only I got away with it". There's the Cash who wrote and sang Tennessee classics *Hey Porter* and *Cry, Cry, Cry* which will linger for ever in America's soul and the Cash who's king of early rock, partner to Carl (Blue Suede Shoes) Perkins in the Midwest's travelling rock'n'roll showcases. And there's Cash who sings songs to his mother, sings with is wife, who keeps faith with his friends and scorns the glitter of success.'

The same publication explains his singing success as lying primarily in his 'stubborn resurrection of a lost art: the story song. He sings with the blunt violence of a tale told first-hand; his artfully spare accompaniment strips the outline of a song to its bare and lonely heart. In *I Walk The Line,* his low-keyed ode to fidelity, and his wife June Carter's own *Ring Of Fire,* it's a heart of dark clarity, a heart that knows definitely that not all of the world is sweetness and light, rainbows and pots of gold.'

He has been accused of singing off-key and the themes of which he sings such as railroads and hobos are hardly in the real memory of listeners. To most people however, Cash himself seems to sing from experience and if he sings of people and times beyond their experience they can still relate to the feelings expressed.

Cash grew up in the traditional manner of country artists, knowing hunger, poverty and the personal tragedy of seeing his brother killed in an accident on the farm. The toughness of his earlier life frequently reveals itself in the songs he writes, songs of floods, broken love affairs, gunfights and Indians. Cash was a kid and young man during the period of the American Depression. He picked cotton, 250 pounds a day, dragging a 9-foot sack down the tangled rows. He would later drag two 5-gallon water jugs to the levee work gangs on the banks of the Tyronza River.

He joined the US Air Force when he was eighteen. He was trained as a radio-interceptor operator and served some of his time in Germany where he purchased his first guitar. He reached the position of staff sergeant and was demobilised after serving four years.

He went to the city. He sold electrical appliances and with time to spare he took a radio announcer's course. At the back of his mind was the thought of becoming a singer. He had entertained his service pals and this had given him the impetus to try his luck in the professional world. Three times he tried for an audition with the famous Sun Records which boasted famous names including Elvis, Conway Twitty, Jerry Lee Lewis, Roy Orbison and Carl Perkins. In the end Sun signed Cash. His first 45 *Cry, Cry, Cry* sold 100,000 and by the third, *I Walk The Line,* he was hitting the million mark. America had a new star, soon to conquer the world. Paul David in his informative book *New Life In Country Music* remarks that Cash sold 6,000,000 records in 1970 alone. Not one of his albums sold less than 100,000 and that figure could be multiplied many times for most records. Cash was in demand but the man who sang *Don't Take Your Guns To Town, The Ballad of Ira Hayes* and *I Still Miss Someone,* was finding his schedules exhausting. From 1960 to 1967 his drug problem grew worse with every passing year. He was locked into the vicious circle of soft drugs, needing stimulants to maintain his emotional energy – then tranquillisers to combat the effects of the stimulants. It was reported in 1965 that he had been arrested at the Mexican border carrying 1,163 pills and he spent a night in El Paso jail. The court gave him a suspended thirty-day sentence and fined him $1,000. He was taking 100 stimulants a day. His first marriage creaked and collapsed. He was in prison again in 1967 and recalls 'I woke up in jail in Georgia and I don't remember how I got there!'

He began to get a reputation for late arrival at concerts and perhaps this was when he decided that something must be done. Help of a real and substantial kind was at hand. In 1968 he had married June Carter, the youngest daughter of Maybelle Carter, a legend in her own right and famed particularly in folk circles during the 1920s and 1930s. Cash said he had kicked the pill habit for good. His new-found stability brought a greater measure of commitment to his profession and he became involved with a weekly show on ABC-TV that was to increase his popularity across the family audience. He swept five awards at the year's Country Music Association's Award Show, an unheard of success. These were indeed new times for Cash.

But more was to come. The influence of June, her family associations and a steadily building relationship with the evangelist Billy Graham led Cash to commit his life to Christ. 'As I grow older, I've grown closer to Him, and if I have a problem now, I take it to Him. He always works it out for me.'

Cash became a father and shortly before his son's birth, Billy Graham visited the family. Cash commented 'He's a good friend of mine and has prayed for me a lot. I also told Billy Graham that the greatest humilation I've suffered was worth it if my example can keep just one person from touching drugs. Now I'm going to build a chapel to the Lord in my home town of Hendersonville (near Nashville) to show Him how much I appreciate the way He has seen fit to bless me ... The name of the Lord is as commonplace in the Cash home as black-eyed peas on their dinner table.'

In 1972 the Gardner-Webb College conferred on him the honorary degree of Doctor of Humanities. It was recognition of the social and humanitarian work Cash had done over the years for the plight of Red Indians, improved conditions in American prisons and his deep concern for the losers and the less fortunate in American society.

But it was the fruits of his new religious commitment that to a large degree shaped the years ahead. In 1969, Bob Dylan had his album *Nashville Skyline* released. Cash sings a duet with Bob on the album entitled *Girls From The North Country*. He gave the US rock star the album title and wrote the sleeve notes. Dylan spent some time in the Cash household. The magazine *Contemporary Christian Music* reported Cash as remarking at the time of Dylan's conversion to Christianity, 'I knew he was searching for the truth and had been for years. And anyone who really wants to find the truth ends up at Jesus.'

Since the 1970s, Cash has continued his music career but has also been involved in several major religious projects. He wrote and produced the film *Gospel Road*. He wrote his own spiritual biography in *Man in Black* and has said he would like to write another musical which would be based on the life of Paul.

To a British person Cash is typical of the American South, an area that has little in common with the rest of America. Cash – like others from the South – has the air of someone for whom religion is common as breathing. But Cash has lifted himself out of the formal acknowledgement into a living experience of his Lord. He is a powerful man who has met life head-on and survived. He says that even though there were years when outwardly he slipped away from his Lord there was still with him the feeling that he could find the Way because he had once seen the Light. It was this inner feeling that compelled him to seek a real commitment to the truth and to share this through his work with anyone who will accept the living relationship that is available with Jesus.

Cash finds a place in this book because he is an important figure in overall rock history. He finds a place because he is the sort of artist and figure who could easily find his way into the general pop arena once more, even though he is no longer a young man. Cash had the presence to dominate, the voice to compel.

Dion

They told this story in the 1950s. The New York IRT subway came to a halt at a Bronx station, and four young men got aboard. They sat down and pulled copies of music from their pockets. A moment later, they were harmonizing a current hit. The few passengers in the car glanced their way and smiled as they switched to a tender ballad. The group was Dion and the Belmonts. In a short space of time they moved on from earning money by singing in the subway to become one of the most famous groups of the late 1950s and early 1960s. Some of their songs became classic pop numbers. The group found greater success in the USA than Britain and Dion was to achieve greater chart triumphs as a solo artist. He was to be billed by CBS as a 'handsome young star of records and most recently of television and motion picture.'

When he emerged on the music scene he was a curly-headed teenager with an equally young group. But music and stage were very much part of his upbringing. His dad was an entertainer and young Dion had made his professional debut at the age of eleven on the Paul Whiteman radio show. He had been singing since the age of five and had begun strumming the guitar soon after.

He and his group took their name from Belmont Avenue in the Bronx. They mixed their talent for singing in an attractive manner with touches of comedy. His own name was real, the christian name, and to say Dion Dimuci seemed a mouthful for fast talking DJ's on the New York airwaves. His parents were called Pat and Frances.

A talent-spotter from Laurie Records noticed the way in which kids reacted to his singing at the local rock 'n' roll show. He made one solo record, and associated himself for a while with the Timberlanes before forming The Belmonts from neighborhood friends. Laurie expert Gene Schwartz knew he — the company — the group — were all into something good. There was a future.

Within a few years Dion and the Belmonts had the kids of the 1950s racing to their record shops. There were hits like *I Wonder Why, A Teenager In Love* (covered successfully in the UK by Marty Wilde) and *Where Or When*.

It was a far cry from the lack of interest shown in Dion's first record *The Chosen Few*. But he had his doubts at the time. 'When we finished that session (the first with the Belmonts) I didn't figure anything could or would happen with the record. But oh, how I longed for it to make it!'

He remembers the first time he heard a record of his own on the radio. 'Can you imagine what it's like to hear your record on the air for the first time? It caught me completely unprepared. It was early in the morning, and I was in the kitchen making myself a bowl of cereal. The radio was turned down low, just so I would catch the weather and the time — then I heard it. My record! I stopped dead still for a second, then I ran over and turned it up. At first I wasn't sure — but when I was I turned it up louder and LOUDER!

'"Mom! Dad!" I yelled. "Come and hear it! Get up and come and hear it! Hurry — Donna! Joan!"'

By the time his parents arrived the record had finished and after their initial disappointment Dion and his parents laughed and hugged. Within minutes the phone was ringing as friends and neighbours called to say they had heard the Dimuci boy!

The early sixties were the years in which he made his

name and earned his place in rock 'n' roll history. Towards the latter part of the decade he became a solo artist and had fourteen titles in Billboard's Top 40 listings nine of which made the top ten. He toured the UK and was given a warm reception but he only had three British hits, *Lonely Teenager, Runaround Sue* and *The Wanderer*. The UK market did not respond to such titles as *Lovers Who Wander, Ruby Baby, Donna The Prima Donna* and *Abraham, Martin and John.*

Suddenly though chart success ended and there was nothing for five long years. Even then his return was limited to one US hit, *Abraham, Martin and John,* but he continued to attract audiences and was far from forgotten.

During this period Dion redefined his musical identity and style. After his success with *Abraham, Martin and John* he left Laurie and signed with Warner Bros, for whom he recorded a well-received album, *Sit Down Old Friend*. He had now changed from a teen idol to a folk poet. The change was complete when he appeared in December 1969 at the Fillmore East, New York.

In 1971 he appeared at a folk festival at Bardney, Lincolnshire. His music was white country blues, relaxed and effortless. The songs had a sensitivity that was the very opposite of the brash style of earlier years when the 'doo wop chorus, the claps, the subway harmonies behind his plaintive, slurred tenor' had suited the times.

He had not entirely rejected the past and the song *The Stuff I Got* recalled old times. Of those earlier days he said, 'I liked the music, I dug it, I was having fun with it. It moved, the sounds were different, and I always experimented in the studios.'

His fans loyally remembered old times too. In 1976 *The Wanderer* hit the charts again in the UK and the record stores found that the hits of the late fifties and early sixties were being bought again, often by fans who had not heard them at all first time round.

By 1975 he was recording with the old maestro himself, Phil Spector. His album, *Born To Be With You* was issued on the Phil Spector International label and it seemed it would only be a matter of time before he recaptured his earlier success. He played with an impressive array of musicians including Nino Tempo, Jim Horn, Bobby Keyes, Barney Kessel and Klaus Voorman. He had released thirty-two albums since 1958 but did not find stardom again.

The years of adulation and worldwide travel left him with an uneasy feeling of dissatisfaction and lack of fulfilment. He realised that there was more to life than owning and being owned by possessions, but he did not know what. He recognised the transitory nature of the music world and how fickle were the audiences. He fell into the booze and drugs trap and towards the end of the sixties, shortly before the success of *Abraham, Martin and John* he was fighting serious drug and alcohol addiction.

Years earlier he had tried to find God. He said, 'I wasn't too close to God in '61. I was confused — maybe well-meaning. I was always a seeker and I wanted to find a better way to express myself.' But he added, 'I looked in a lot of wrong places.'

Now he turned to God again. It was the beginning of a spiritual awakening. 'When I wanted to turn my life to Him, He removed my drug and alcohol problem. I knew that God is real. I began to know Him as my Father. But I still didn't understand Jesus.' In fact, his concept of God was vague at that time.

It was years later that he came to a deeper understanding. He identifies 14 December 1979 as the day of his conversion. In conversation with Christian writer Dan Wooding he recalled how he had been running away from all kinds of things, such as the pressure of so many people depending on him. He described his surprise when a neighbour asked him about his reaction to Jesus. The man told him 'Dion, Jesus has done a lot for me.' Dion told Dan, 'I stopped right there. What did he mean by that? What did Jesus do anyway?'

That day he stopped running away from himself and from God but it took him eleven years to become what he termed 'a man of prayer and faith', feeling a real closeness to God. 'I said "God I'd like to be closer to you". And I guess it's like the Bible says "Ask and ye shall receive", you know?' Suddenly things became clearer. He began to see why Jesus has been such an important figure down the ages. When Karen Marie Platt of *Contemporary Christian* asked if he had been born again Dion replied emphatically, 'Oh, definitely. Brand-new. The old passes away.' He said he knew beyond any measure of doubt that Jesus had changed his heart. In 1980 he told Karen that he wanted to share on a personal level what God had done with his life. He had no idea if he would perform and sing on the general music scene in the future. He said, 'I don't know about tomorrow. I make some plans and God works it out His own way.'

He signed with the Christian record company Word. *Inside Job* and *Only Jesus* were his two first recordings. *Inside Job* reflected the phrase 'blind now I see' while *Only Jesus* stimulates 'a joy to the Lord'. In his third album *I Put Away My Idols* he sang of the power, nature and depth of God and how they are predominant in Scripture.

He said he had travelled all over the world and found God's love and truth so wonderful. He was excited by the many ways in which God works. 'My new career has been an exciting way of sharing with people what God is doing for me in my life, in the best way I know how . . . through my music and song.'

To many Dion is still living out his hit, *The Wanderer*. He hopes his new record ministry will change that!

Leon Patillo

It created quite a paradox when Leon Patillo joined the group Santana as vocalist and keyboard player. Patillo was a commited Christian while Carlos Santana, founder of the group, was a disciple of the guru Sri Chinmoy. Despite their different views, or perhaps because they both had a strong religious commitment, they became good friends.

Leon came from a family that attended church although his parents were of different denominations. Young Leon was encouraged musically and he even began to re-arrange familiar church hymns in a style that drew quite a crowd of young people. The church's pastor didn't find it to his liking.

'At the time I was relating to God the best way I knew — through the music He'd put inside of me. I tried to explain that to the pastor, but he couldn't go along with it.'

Leon turned from the church and music claimed his attention. Soon he was playing professionally in the Bay area. He went down to Los Angeles where there was a great deal of recording and Martha Reeves, the well-known Motown artist, asked him to conduct for her and the Vandellas. He learned quickly and soon he was asked to work with the popular outfits Rare Earth, and Funkadelic who became Parliament. Rare Earth had come from Detroit and charted in pop soul with their hybrid of funky blues, soul and hard rock. Parliament had had a US top 40 smash *(I Wanna) Testify*.

Patillo wrote a great deal and to his surprise he kept

coming up with religious lyrics – at least God kept popping up. 'It was as though my upbringing in the church just wouldn't let me go.' A song called *Keep The Spirit* was particularly personal. It was about the Holy Spirit seemingly searching, probing and directing his work. He recalls a line in the song 'Must, must be Someone' and reflected how 'it actually provoked a kind of faith in me, and at times I cried when I sang it.'

He realised that this feeling was not common to every-one and some of the group even suggested that his sparkle and smile were perhaps a reflection of drug-taking. There was drug taking. It was expected that groups would be smashed out of their minds before they played, often for audiences who had spent hours smoking pot or taking acid.

Carlos Santana was a Mexican musician who spent his formative years in Tijuana and then, during the late sixties, in the Haight-Ashbury area of San Francisco. Carlos became closely involved with the teachings of guru Sri Chinmoy through fellow musician John McLaughlin. The two disciples released an album entitled *Love* in 1974 and Carlos subsequently collaborated with another disciple, Alice Coltrane, on an album called *Illuminations*. Mean-while in his own rock group his influence was shaped by his mystical world view.

He was the guest singer on the album *The Live Adventures Of Mike Bloomfield And Al Kooper* and gradually his fame extended, with a series of albums under the name Santana, musically a mix of cosmic, psychedelic strains with jazz and Latin influences. The *Rolling Stone Illustrated History of Rock & Roll* described his music, 'There was the standard rock drummer, but there was also a timbales player on percussion. The rhythms were tight, metallic and Latin, the guitar cast in a jazz and Hendrix vein. The lugubrious, been-stoned-too-long lethargy that the old psychedelic bands had fallen into was completely absent; Santana was as tight and sharp as a patent leather shoe.'

A series of fine albums preceded Leon's involvement with Carlos Santana, although some critics felt that his best work was completed before 1974. However, the Patillo — Santana association was a powerful one. Leon was asked to join the group and tour England and Japan. 'Even though Carlos' Buddhist beliefs conflicted with my own conviction that Eastern religions were way off the track, we became like brothers,' Leon said.

Carlos had engaged Leon for his vocals. He was unaware of his writing abilities, but they were quickly appreciated. Santana released two albums *Borboletta* and *Festival*. On the first Leon sings vocals on tracks *Practice What You Preach, Mirage* (lyrics and music his), *Life Is A New* and *One With The Sun*. He also contributed piano. On *Festival* he shared song credits with Carlos, Tom Coster and David Rubinson but alone wrote the penultimate cut *Try A Little Harder*. The album came wrapped in an inner and outer sleeve that reflected Carlos' religious faith.

But Leon Patillo was a Christian. He made his commitment in 1974 at a Christian coffee bar in his home city of San Francisco. It was just before the group's European tour. Someone had approached him and suggested that he might like to attend a Christian meeting. 'Somehow I knew my number was up!' He was confronted by the Gospel that he had pushed aside when he stopped going to church. It was a struggle to surrender to Christ – he thought about 'the money, the parties, the girls and the dope and the prestige' but the girl who spoke at the coffee bar talked of the difference between things of the flesh and those of the Spirit. It made him aware of his inner loneliness, that he had never realised his full potential simply because he had not seen his life in the light and truth of the Christian faith. That night a new Patillo was born.

'Jesus was saving me from all that (drugs etcetera) for a life of true fulfilment.' It had immediate effect for he ran home and wrote five songs!

The split with Santana had to come though at first Carlos did not see why Leon's Christian faith might cause problems. There was to be a brief reunion in 1976 when Leon was asked to contribute material and sing on the *Festival* album. To his surprise his songs were accepted, even though they were grounded in his new beliefs.

'We wrote one song together called *The River*. Carlos tried to write about his mystical spiritual experiences and I tried to make the song about Jesus. He would start singing about "consciousness", then I would try to zero in on who really is the source of life. Finally, I was able to keep asserting the words that focussed the song on Jesus, and the end result was a love song about Christ, the creator of life.' But when Carlos asked him later to participate in another album Leon said no. This time he felt he received a different direction from the Lord.

His Christian convictions were soon known and as he says 'Had I not been in Santana I couldn't have spoken to such people as Peter Frampton, Eric Clapton, The Bee Gees and Earth, Wind and Fire. The Lord had me there for a specific purpose at that time.' He told Wesley Want of America's *Keystone* magazine how one evening at the Roxy club in Hollywood he gathered together fellow believers including Syreeta, Deneice Williams and Philip Bailey and invited all kinds of people from the music business. The word got around that there would be gospel music and an incredible motley crowd of stars, musicians, actresses and actors arrived. Many responded to the Gospel that evening, amongst them the famous Donna Summer. She opened her studio to Leon and whoever would come, and fortnightly Bible studies were held. It was an evening when the recording desk was silent and no one needed to feed music into an artist's cans.

Leon completed a three-year Bible study programme in twelve months and married Jackie who took on responsibility for his bookings and personal appearances.

Leon developed a solo career and *Dance Children Dance* was released in 1979 for Maranatha! Music. In 1980 and 1981 he toured extensively outside the United States. He signed with the Christian label Myrrh and they released *Don't Give Up*. Then to his delight he and Jackie had a son, Gabriel. Philip Bailey, even Carlos, and production from ace man Skip Konte helped him on his next album *I'll Never Stop Lovin' You*.

The foundations for the style of his solo act were laid during a tour of Australia. He filled the stage with the most advanced electronic keyboards and synthesizers available. Playing a Yamaha CP70, the Oberheim Ob-Xa, the DSX Digital Polyphonic Sequenser and DMS Programmable Drum machine, he produced the sound of a full band plus a symphonic orchestra! His albums *Live Experience* (an in-concert affair) and *The Sky's The Limit* extended his music ministry and, because he is known for his professionalism, his career has grown beyond the limits that can exist when a singer is under contract to a religious label.

Dan Peek

Dirt Pit Manor was formerly used as a cowman's house but during the early years of the group America it was home.

There were three guys in the group. Dewey Bunnel, had been born in England. He and Gerry Beckley had British mothers and American fathers. The group's third member Dan Peek was one hundred per cent American. All were sons of American servicemen in Britain.

Peek was from Florida. He had learnt the guitar from an early age, and was proficient as a guitarist and vocalist when he was twelve. With the others he attended the Central High School in Bushey, and on one occasion they turned down a European tour with the Byrds because they said they had been booked by their school for some concerts!

They had come to Britain around 1966 and when their fathers retired and returned home the three decided they would rather stay here. Dan, in fact, returned home to Virginia for a year while Gerry and Dewey worked together in an electronic group but America was reunited in 1968. Their musical empathy was excellent for as Gerry put it at the time, 'We just discovered we had all been writing and it all came together – the result is what we are now.'

The tangible result was a single *A Horse With No Name* that became a monster smash hit and is still played and regarded as a pop classic. Nothing else was to prove as successful in Britain although *Ventura Highway* just made the British top 50. In their own country the group had nine top 40 hits between March 1972 and the summer of 1976 and six of those made the top ten. Those big top ten smashes included *Horse With No Name, I Need You, Ventura Highway, Tin Man, Lonely People* and *Sister Golden Hair.*

The guys were puzzled by the difference in chart fortunes. 'We don't really know why' was Dewey's comment. However, Britain had provided their inspiration. Dan remembers the golden days of British music. 'There's no doubt that British rock music led the world in the 60s with the Beatles, the Stones, the Who and countless others. They influenced us and to be there in the country where they were raised and started was something.'

The success of *A Horse With No Name* rather caught them and others unaware. The group were opposed to singles since they felt a hit single could often limit a band's style by representing a very small part of their total range. Initially they were uncertain of the song's hit potential. They felt it was record company policy that dictated release. In Britain the industry's argument is simple. Album material gets little time on the air so the way to attract attention to it is by issuing one or two singles with material from the album. People who like the single will buy the album. And the method works.

The group developed musically as its popularity grew. They considered percussion early, recognising a definite need to augment the acoustic guitars for stage performance. A musician called Ray Cooper was very much under consideration in early times and he had played on their recordings.

But there was a problem in extending the group beyond a trio. 'There's a basic personality thing which is very hard for anyone who might join this band to get over. All three of us are so close as musicians and people. We live together, play together, work together, do everything together.'

They also thought of everything including electric guitars but they lacked capital. Drums came into their thinking and the obvious candidate was from their old group The Daze who had played on their debut album. And visually they thought that more could be achieved.

Gigs were played with The Who, Family, Cat Stevens, Elton John and a host of others until they eventually headlined. The album *America* was followed by *Homecoming, Holiday* and *Hat-Trick*. A single *Mad Dog And Tin Man* prefaced release of their fifth album in which, as for *Holiday,* production and musical arrangement was by George Martin. The group penned the songs, added three back-up singers and had the title track of the movie *The Story Of A Teenager.*

Their brand of easy-on-the-ear soft rock had captured a wide ranging audience. 'Our audiences were all ages, descriptions, all shapes and sizes. Our strength lay in songwriting.' Dan's contribution in the songwriting department came in songs such as *Don't Cross The River, Today's The Day, Lonely People* and *Women Tonight.*

Through the 1970s in America, the group had won the 1972 Grammy Award, played to full houses during thirty-two statewide tours, headlined three world tours and made countless radio and television appearances. The blow came when Dan said he was leaving. It was 1977. Here he was a rich man, loved by thousands of fans, still knowing chart triumphs. Yet he chose to leave the band with nothing particular in mind, musically.

'I came to realize that spiritually I was flat broke.' He had become increasingly conscious of this since his wife became a Christian in 1976. They had married three years previously. Dan had always thought of himself as influenced by Christianity but faced by the positive testimony of his wife's life he became conscious that nominal Christian living is only a pale shadow of the real thing. He was also aware that his musical career had interrupted any spiritual growth. Life had become too cluttered, too oriented towards preserving and ensuring records sold, tours were sell-outs and basically keeping the group at the top against the continual influx of stiff competition.

He remembers one point during the seventies when he made a prayer which in hindsight was more of an attempted bargaining gambit than saying 'Thy will be done.' He recalls praying 'Lord, if you'll make this thing work, I'll give you all the glory and use it as a platform for you.' But he didn't! There were too many diversions. He even recoiled from writing and singing religious material in case it alienated the fans. 'With a mind fogged by drugs' and a feeling that he was really controlled at all levels by career and record demands he knew deep down that he must really take charge of his own life.

This would mean leaving the group America, the band he had nurtured and the other two who were his close friends. Furthermore, any decision he made would affect the other two drastically. Yet he felt he must dedicate himself 100 per cent to the Lord and he felt he could not do so by remaining within the musical fold.

He found it hard to say that he wanted out. So he began missing rehearsals and consequently causing problems and a general build-up of apprehension and frustration in those affected. Finally Gerry and Dewey asked him if he wanted out and when the answer was yes this part of his life came to a close.

For a while he had ideas of recording an album of songs that were about Jesus. Not unexpectedly the powers that be thought it was not a commercial proposition. However, this didn't deter Dan from believing that he must use his musical awareness for telling the Gospel. Eventually he recorded an album *All Things Are Possible* for Pat Boone's Lamb & Lion label.

Dan knew he would pay heavily for worshipping his ego over the years. He had built his life on finances and possessions, he had grown up on an American 'ethic in which making money becomes a goal. I figured that whatever I lacked in my personality could be made up by money.' But he realized those who make big money usually lust for more and then more. He knew money could not satisfy the needs deep down inside his soul.

Only Jesus could do that. Thankfully, he realised it.

Richie Furay

'Richie Furay has been one of the guardian angels of rock music over the past five years' said the British musical weekly *Sounds* in 1972.

Within two years he was needing guardian angels amongst the American music press. Furay had rejected the drug-ridden rock era of the late 1960s and early 1970s and had become a Christian. Some journalists forgot his music but focused instead on deriding his faith. They looked no further than the very thing they did not understand.

Furay first proclaimed his beliefs in a very bold feature in a leading US monthly *Crawdaddy,* which examines and analyses the state of rock music and musicians. Having brought together the Souther-Hillman-Furay Band Billy was very much in the news when the magazine was celebrating its 30th birthday. He was asked to contribute a feature on their special issue. Furay gave a bold Christian testimony complete with biblical references. He called it 'A Good Feeling To Know'. It was published on the same page as 'Flying Saucers Rock'n'Roll', by rock's flamboyant 'tell you what life is' (usually without hope) Patti Smith.

Furay couldn't have attracted more attention and the fury to Furay rang across newspaper and magazine offices. Furay recalls how *Crawdaddy's* editor warned him that the public announcement could well ruin his career or at least severely damage his future. It was to do just that, as some record people were unhappy with the kind of faith-based lyrics that he began to write and the songs he wanted to sing but Furay was determined to lose the old image.

Furay had achieved the *Sounds'* acknowledgement by being part of the influential rock era of music that had begun around 1967. In New York he was with the Au Go Go Singers (that included Stephen Stills), with whom he recorded one album and made numerous TV appearances. He met up with Stills again in California on the West Coast and he joined with Neil Young, Bruce Palmer and Dewey Morgan to form Buffalo Springfield.

The band was before its time with its material and its eclectic country-rock style became widely influential on the groups that stormed the music world toward the end of the 1960s. Often the music was sheer delight. There was a magical chemistry and on the best, the debut album Furay's countryish vocals were prominent.

For What It's Worth, an early protest song, was the only big hit from the album although the music critics praised it highly. On the second album, *Buffalo Springfield Again* the musicianship and production stole the ear. By the release of their third record *Last Time Around* the group was hardly functioning any more. A superb composition by Furay on this album, *Kind Woman,* was acknowledged by US journal *Rolling Stone* as the 'first rock number to feature pedal steel guitar.'

Furay, based in Los Angeles, formed Poco in 1968. He was joined by another ex-Springfield musician Jim Messina. Poco became another legendary outfit with an enormous following. At first Poco was Pogo (perhaps foreseeing the 'punk' era!) but after they received a writ from Walt Kelly, creator of the comic strip bearing the same name, it was definitely Poco. Furay was still contracted to Atlantic but finally was released by them to record with Poco on the Epic label. The debut album *Pickin' Up The Pieces* sold 100,000 and three albums were released before Furay wanted out and had other things in mind – the Souther-Hillman-Furay band.

A great many of Furay's songs in those days were about the traditional boy-girl relationship. Furay says he was not politically oriented and he had no solution to offer on that front. In talking about the Buffalo Springfield times he admits that he and the others were young and naive. They were defenceless against what he terms 'vultures that were trying to lead us this way or lead us that way and it was really really difficult for us.' Later he felt pleased when it was acknowledged that Buffalo Springfield laid the foundations for much exciting music that followed.

The music press in the early 1970s suggested that Furay was well into the music but like most artists he had his share of disappointment. He was rather discouraged by the low level of interest in the first Poco album that extended – so he felt – even into the record's promotion. He felt they were 'not pushed right ... needed more help at the beginning.' As the band hit the road the musical journals showed more interest but the late 1960s and early 1970s were rife with numerous fine groups and bands competing for press coverage, airplay and sales.

In 1975 he became a Christian and a year later he recorded *I've Got A Reason*. The album was ignored. The born-again Richie had to pay the price forecast by the editor of *Crawdaddy*.

In 1981 it was re-issued and the advertising blurb said,

'the music industry was caught off guard (by the album). But not the fans who had heard of his conversion and bought the record. They found in the album the same professional musical talent that had produced the chart-topping single *For What It's Worth* in the 60s with Buffalo Springfield; the same fluid vocals that had netted Richie Furay several gold albums with his own country-rock band in the 70s. But they also found a sensitive, fresh statement of the exciting renewal in Richie's own life. It was an album ahead of its time.'

The original release of *I've Got A Reason* on Asylum was followed by two solo albums *Dance A Little Light* and *I Still Have Dreams*. He said, 'I gave Asylum more of what they wanted, so they would support me; and then, I could do what I wanted to do. In the meantime, it just didn't happen. It wasn't what God wanted to happen.' The re-issue was on the Myrrh label, part of the Word record company. His contract with them also allowed him to continue exploring secular outlets.

The two worlds came together in a dramatic fashion at the end of 1980. Furay formed United States Rock. He saw the band as a Christian-based rock outfit that would be musically more than acceptable and at the same time would witness in the group's lyrics to Christ. It was not to be. He was advised against the project and he himself came to feel it was not God's will to continue.

'I'm a servant of the Lord, and that's by choice. I'm a bondslave by choice. I love the Lord because He first loved me. Nobody broke my arms to do it.'

He recorded another album for Myrrh entitled *Seasons of Change*. Today he sees life in terms of what it means to follow Jesus. 'I have to be an example of that way'.

It's far from the Richie Furray of the 1960s but he hasn't looked back . . .

Singer-Songwriters, Producers

Bryn Haworth

Bryn had something bulging out of his back pocket. It was a well-thumbed Bible. It goes everywhere with this fine musician and song-writer who has accompanied the stars and released solo albums.

He was eleven when he had his first guitar. His father made sure that he learnt properly, none of this three-chord folk stuff! Rock was his abiding musical interest and so he found himself a group. He played long into the night at clubs but found employment hard since he was frequently late for work.

He moved to London from the North-West where he grew up for the city draws artists like a magnet, mainly because the record companies and the music press are there.

Bryn joined Fleur de Lys, a Mod band. After leaving that he went to the US where he toured with a band called Wolfgang, whose claim to fame was supporting Zeppelin.

Meanwhile, he began writing songs and after getting an encouraging response from friends he decided on his return to London to try and interest some record companies. Island seemed a good one, for it produced quite a few artists with a progressive and intimate style. Several interesting albums came from this association. They had some good songs and you felt Haworth was sincere and uncompromising. In 1973 he released *Let The Days Go By*, then *Sunny Side Of The Street* and for A&M, *Grand Arrival* and *Keep The Ball Rolling*. These albums reflected his

Christian faith. They also displayed his tremendous ability on the guitar. He collaborated and worked with artists including Richie Hayward, the drummer of Little Feat; expatriate Liverpool singer Jackie Lomax, sessions for Joan Armatrading, Andy Fairweather Low, Gerry Rafferty, Pete Wingfield, Cliff Richard and many others.

His guitar forte became slide (or bottleneck) guitar, a technique derived from the blues and elevated into a tradition by the likes of Robert Johnson, Muddy Waters, Bukka White, Eric Clapton, Duane Allman and Lowell George. Bryn developed a distinctive style which explains why he has often been in demand. Roger Hill writing for *New Music* wrote 'he seeks not to imitate the ominous quality of Waters, or the frenetic attack of Elmore James, or the piercing sting of Lowell George, discovering instead a gentler approach which sounds like nobody else and which beautifully complements his highly melodic songs.'

During his time in the US he met a beautiful girl called Sally. He changed his mind about being part of a big rock outfit and decided to settle in Wales with Sally. It was at a time when he felt self-assured, 'very cocky' and 'just enjoying the whole ride. You know the power you've got over people and you play up to it. It was a childish thing.'

Unlike many people, Bryn started to search for religious certainties because life was so good, rather than because it was so bad. He had a lot going for him and he felt that because he had fulfiled himself in so many ways, he might now search for God. Sally was involved in a similar spiritual challenge but she was attracted to the Krishna community and there was a period when she spent the waking day busily chanting Krishna to herself.

Next to their home in Wales there was a church, rather small and attractive. Perhaps it's presence encouraged Bryn to write the song *Grappenhall Rag* that opens with the line 'I believe in him'. Later he said the line did not represent any personal awareness of Jesus, if anything it merely represented his search for someone, somebody who could give him answers to the deep questions he was asking.

He and Sally married and returned to her home state of California. Bryn toured as support to the likes of Traffic and Fairport Convention. One night he had a strange experience. He sensed that the audience did not really appreciate either his musical ability or him personally and he experienced an overwhelming sense of loneliness. To the side of the stage he suddenly saw a figure which gave him comfort. Later he enquired who had come on stage but no one could give any answer. Bryn believed it was the Lord. He wrote in his notebook 'Now I really know God is with me.' From this moment a greater certainty grew which affected Sally as well.

Later, back in the UK, he was painting a circus tent and while driving down to Eastbourne he saw one that looked identical. He and Sally went along expecting a circus! They arrived and instead of clowns and animals, sawdust and bright lights, they found a choir and a banner proclaiming that Jesus was the one who said 'I am the way, the truth and the life.' It was a mission led by evangelist Dick Saunders.

Saunders made an appeal. Sally felt compelled to go forward. Bryn wasn't so keen but plenty of time was given and he eventually followed. It was his time of true commitment when he fully gave himself to the Lord. He remembers being counselled, but overriding the spoken words was a marvellous sensation that things were alright. He told Garth Hewitt during one of his rare interviews, 'And I thought. "Yeah I'm in the plan now, I'm in His hands". That's all I remember, the beautiful sky – it all fitted.'

Bryn also told Garth how he found being a Christian.

'It's so important to be yourself, to be natural. I have been frightened talking about the Lord, like if I'm writing a song and it's half-finished, and it's about him, I think "How am I going to record·this? They won't like it". But nobody lynches you, nobody bothers. The devil has a stage so the Lord can have a stage. Nobody is going to lynch you. Pray to be strong for him and talk to people naturally about the Lord. Don't worry if they don't understand. It's how it comes out from you. It's got to be natural. People want to know if there is a God.'

And how does Bryn communicate as a Christian and a musician?

In another interview with Garth, Bryn commented 'My responsibility is to communicate how God thinks and feels. To encourage, build-up and strengthen people in faith and truth and love, and to work heartily at serving the Lord ... some people would feel their job is just to make good records and that's fine too, but I'm trying to tell people the whole truth of God.'

He mentioned something else that all Christians can forget – that is the necessity of the discipline of a daily quiet time, a definite period of Bible study. 'It's the last thing a rock'n'roll musician wants to hear. We've spent most of our lives being undisciplined – doing what we want.'

His musical ministry has taken him into definite Christian areas and he does not feel uncomfortable playing in the mixed nature of a Christian gathering. He recorded an album *The Gap* for Chapel Lane in which he kept his individualism using it to make songs with very positive spiritual lyrics.

In his quiet way he is leading many to know the truth he feels deeply – Jesus is the true way to God.

Arlo Guthrie

Write an epic song and you can never escape from it! So reads the Arlo Guthrie story.

The singer-songwriter was one of several children born to Woody Guthrie and his wife Marjorie. Woody became the American folk figure of the 1930s and 1940s and the inspiration for US folk greats Pete Seeger and, later, folk-rock legend, Bob Dylan. Arlo was born in 1947 on Coney Island, New York. He was reared in music – it seemed as natural that he should learn the guitar and sing as he should eat and he was playing competently at the age of six!

A famous father may be welcome in some ways but in others it can be handicap and it was not until Arlo's epic eighteen-minute hit *Alice's Restaurant* in 1967 that he was able to escape from being introduced as 'Woody's son' and recognised in his own right. The song was very much tongue-in-cheek; it was amusing and perceptive, a story song about prevailing social conditions of the time. It cocked a snook at the establishment and became an American campus student favourite at a time when young and old were estranged over their attitude to life.

He recorded countless other story songs, often on subjects beyond the pale for chart singles. He never avoided any difficult subject nor was he particularly worried if what he said went against the grain. *Coming Into Los Angeles* became the dope-smuggling anthem and most popular song from the album *Running Down The Road*. His interpretation of Steve Goodman's *City Of New Orleans* was the pick of the 1972 album *Hobo's Lullaby*. A plethora of musical and personal influences permeated *Last Of The Brooklyn Cowboys*. The track *Presidential Rag* on the album *Arlo Guthrie* was one of rock's most vehement protests against Richard Nixon. *Children Of Abraham* dealt with the Israeli-Arab disputes in the Middle-East. Chilean poet Victor Jara was one of several to receive his attention on the 1976 album *Amigo*.

The year 1976 was an important year for Arlo. From a Jewish family, Arlo joined a Franciscan community and, as Dylan was later to acknowledge, it was because he saw Jesus as 'the Son of the only God'. In common with the first Christians who were Jews he saw the promises of the Jewish Old Testament being fulfilled in Jesus – that indeed He was the Messah. He has added 'I think when we're baptized we open a door in which the Holy Spirit can enter to teach and lead us, to develop us and form us.'

His religious thoughts and seeking were focused on an album entitled *Outlasting The Blues*. There are songs about faith, family, living in the country and man's mortality. The latter was particularly relevant to Arlo. His father had died from Huntington's Chorea, a hereditary illness which has a 50/50 chance of being passed on to the offspring of any sufferer. It becomes evident in mid-life. He said 'There's a certain value to life that makes it worth living. No matter how long you live or how tall or how short or how big or how wide you are – the value is what I'm interested in. That's what I'm pursuing.'

To him the trail of truth was pre-eminent. 'I want to pierce all the veils. I wanna feel it, taste it, I want to know what the real story is. I like my opinion to always be fresh. I don't want to be stereotyped into a situation that I can't be moved from. I'm just a pilgrim.'

He told writer-journalist Danny Smith how he responded to people who talked of a turning point in their spiritual experience – a moment of faith – and how Christian belief had affected him. 'I cannot relax as a Christian and say now everything's okay. If those guys can do it, fine, that's not my personality. I've not come to this point in my life to put down the thing that I was carrying – I'm still looking for where it goes. That's why I'm not going to sell anybody anything. I'll say I'm really happy to be here. I really love being where I am. At this point in my life, I love being here – it's a real fun base for me to operate from.'

There was a specific time when he felt he could say he was deciding to follow Christ. 'I think I've grown a tremendous amount in my spiritual life because the relationship with God is now mediated by his Son. Before that I was trying to reach an awesome reality on my own.'

Referring to his role and relationship within the Franciscan order he said, 'To be able to provide for the world and its people with the gifts of God, one must learn to be a vehicle for these things of God. In that way, Franciscans provide God with opportunities to help others and also yourself.'

Guthrie may be an unknown figure to anyone reared in the musical and cultural world of the late 1970s and the 1980s. However, to those of his and the next generation his new found faith challenges them with the question of how they respond to Jesus.

Michael Omartian

Michael Omartian was nineteen when he decided he would pretend to be a Beatle. He adopted the Liverpool mop and wore the mandatory suit that was sported by his four heroes.

He was probably better qualified musically. He had played the accordion at the age of four, the drums at five and had taken to the piano when he was seven. He specialized in keyboards. His Beatle worshipping days were in 1964, the year the fab four got admitted finally to the American record release schedule. The Beatles dominated the American record scene and opened the floodgates for myriads of other British artists. Michael thought the world of them.

He became a Christian in 1965 and went to work with Campus Crusade for Christ, an organization that sponsers Christian activities in colleges and universities. His musical knowledge was put to good use and he worked closely with some of the first Jesus music groups.

By 1969 he was working in the American music business, really learning his craft and finding many ways in which his enormous talent and knowledge could be used to good effect. He learnt production skills, involved himself in session work, arranged songs and even put together a session band.

The list of people he worked with during the 1970s and since reads like one of the all-time great concert billings and with it came major chart successes. At one point in

1972 five of the top 20 singles had either been arranged by him or he had been a principal musician on those discs. Since then he has worked with Christopher Cross, Rod Stewart, Donna Summer, The Four Tops, Gladys Knight, Vikki Carr, Art Garfunkel, Neil Diamond, Johnny Rivers, David Cassidy, Seals and Crofts, Glen Campbell, Steely Dan, Boz Scaggs, Dusty Springfield and many others, including a number of prominant Jesus Music artists.

Throughout his career Michael Omartian has never forgotten his religious faith and reflecting on his life he says, 'I realize that God has given me a talent, but I'll tell you something: everything that's ever happened to me I can honestly say I had nothing to do with. I was just kind of an innocent bystander. It was always like an accident when things would happen like that. That's why I know that God has really ordained the path.'

His own recording career has continued alongside his secular and religious recordings for others. In 1972 he was signed to ABC Records and *White Horse,* his debut album was released in 1974. On it he worked with the love of his life Stormie. Her traumatic childhood had reduced the teenage Stormie to near suicide. Her mother's cruelty made it difficult to believe she could be a normal child. 'She would tell me I was crazy and after a while I'd begin to believe I *was* crazy. I always wished her dead, and I had a lot of guilt because of that. I grew up with this terrible insecure feeling in every cell of my body.'

Eventually she found a niche in show business and her acting skills were used to good effect. In a sense the whole process of stage work related directly to her needs. 'My whole identity was wrapped up in acting. I was crying out for the kind of love that I never got until I met the Lord.' A year after she became a Christian Stormie married fellow believer Michael.

Life was not all straightforward for Stormie had to come

to terms with her earlier experiences and rid herself of the hatred and guilt that surrounded the mother-child relationship. Eventually her new faith gave her the strength and the answers and she could proclaim with a joy born of pain and suffering 'Thank God my identity is in Him.' It wasn't easy for her.

Michael's second album *Adam Again* was issued on the religious label Myrrh. He used some of the finest Los Angeles session men to create a sound which was to introduce a Christian dimension onto the contemporary music scene. The four-part *Telos Suite* on the second side interested many people but it was perhaps less effective than individual songs such as the title cut and a boistrous, triumphant finale *Here He Comes*. The lyrics for the album were written by Stormie as was the satirical *Whachersign* that sent-up those who relied on astrology to direct their lives. *Seasons Of The Soul* and *Builder* were two albums which were aimed at the Christian community, though it was prayed that unbelievers might hear them too.

While Michael's albums have been well received in the Christian market they have not been widely appreciated outside. It's been his work with top rated musical stars that has drawn attention to his faith together with his consumate studio professionalism. The high regard with which he is held in the musical world has won him wide and favourable press coverage, with journalists often mentioning his Christian faith.

His Christian beliefs led to one news story when he insisted on issuing a disclaimer to some of his work with Rod Stewart. While Michael was proud of his arrangements and production he said he did not agree with some of the sexual overtones added by the world famous star. And indeed he has always been careful to preserve the integrity of his faith whether in his general music work or in the various television and film scores that he has written.

He stands as a positive witness to the fact that Christians can embrace first-rate professionalism and unhesitatingly honour their first commitment when it comes down to relating this faith to their work.

T-Bone Burnett

T-Bone Burnett speaks his mind. He does so in interviews and in the lyrics in his albums. His views may challenge the beliefs of some conservative Christians but T-Bone's prior concern is that Christians should really understand what Jesus said, what the Bible says and should not equate the culture in which they live with the true teaching of Scripture. His diatribes have often been directed against his home country where he sees some interpretation of Christianity as depending on the American way of life rather than the Gospel.

He is especially concerned for today's rock audience. His stature in the United States has been growing fast. His first solo album *Truth Decay* in 1980 had a rather limited reception but his 1982 release *Trap Door* was listed by US journal *Rolling Stone* as one of the top 40 offerings of the year.

He has been involved with record producing and writing, and with accompanying other artists. He toured with Bob Dylan when 'Bob's Rolling Thunder Revue' pushed its way across the States in the mid-1970s. As a member in the Alpha Band he took part in the making of three albums.

During the eighties he has toured as support for the Who during their gigantic farewell tour of the US. It gained him enormous audiences and brought him directly to the attention of the music press covering these concerts. His intelligent and perceptive lyrics proved popular with the more thoughtful audiences.

Burnett sees himself 'out there' speaking to and with a great mass of people hungry for truth. He believes in giving them a good shaking-down and not feeding them cultural conceptions, values, prejudices and falsehoods. 'I don't want to rope people in and offer them some candy to tell them about Jesus. I don't think that's right.'

He sees his work in these terms. 'My ministry is to make doubters out of unbelievers.' His chosen path is a hard one for the message he shares can be too challenging for many people. They demand something more comfortable and less complicated. Some of his views might be questioned by fellow Christians but the American singer is quite adamant that he knows the Lord. He says with firmness, 'I am a Christian and I think what I'm doing is healthy.'

Bruce Cockburn

Cockburn is a favourite of thinking Christians. He moves in social-political areas where his audiences often include those who want to see Christian theology and ethics applied to today's culture and shaping western thought. His perceptive lyrics also concern themselves with problems at the level of the individual in a world that is fundamentally insecure. Friendships and family concern him as much as ecological and political matters.

He has been termed a musician's musician and a poet's poet and certainly his success has been restricted. This has partly been due to the nature of recent rock and the overall cultural malaise. It is neither fashionable to criticise a preoccupation with instant gratification nor popular to propose the Christian alternatve.

British music papers of a more serious nature than those simply concerned with popular charts have occasionally mentioned him but only the British monthly *Strait* and the US journal *Contemporary Christian Music* have acclaimed him. The leading US religious journal *Christianity Today* and the journal *Rolling Stone* have also carried articles about him.

His albums have been plentiful though rarely effectively promoted. It's not easy to promote someone like Cockburn. In the late 1970s and the eighties singer-songwriters have not been particularly successful in the area of the more aggressive rock music. Cockburn puts lyrics first in his writing and disciplines himself accordingly. His music expresses his life experiences. His Christian faith is the alternative he has chosen above black magic, dope, Buddhism and dualism after trying and finding these insufficient.

'Gradually I was led to see at first only the merit of Jesus' teaching rather than something that was living and that I could have living in me. Gradually I came to the point where I knew I'd either have to commit myself to Him or pass.

'I saw through getting kicked around some, I wasn't as self-sufficient as I thought. So I stepped over the threshold and got on my knees and asked Him for help. Since then, I have been a Christian. The song that really marks the turning point is *All The Diamonds In The World*.

'Faith for me is always hot and cold, it comes and goes depending on all kinds of things ... my faith is in the music because I try to make the music reflect what I live through.'

While he talks of how the Gospel teaching has imprinted itself so clearly upon his thinking he is also aware that actually seeing, touching and feeling the real situation is important. So he went to Nicaragua and saw and learnt. So his song repertoire grows and equally his ability to communicate. The Christian scene would certainly be poorer without it. Cockburn never avoids the awkward political issues but his interviews have shown that his experiences give him more than superficial understanding. While he deplores the human waste he also speaks of the hope amongst Christians in Nicaragua. He has not allowed himself to lose either objectivity or, perhaps equally important, a sense of humour. An example of this is his song *Peggy's Kitchen Wall*.

Initial interest in Christianity was partly derived from his own wedding. His girlfriend wanted them to marry in church and when the ceremony reached the point where there was an exchange of rings Cockburn became aware of a presence.

'It was very vivid, very tangible and caught me completely by surprise. It wasn't a visual thing – I just knew there was somebody there ... because it was a Christian church I assumed that it had something to do with Christianity. From that point I got more interested and started reading C.S. Lewis and the Bible.'

He does not see himself as a direct evangelist. 'I don't think that's what I have been called to do. Of course, I hope people see that Christianity is an alternative for them as a result of hearing my music, but I am approaching it from a different place. I'm not trying to sell Christianity. I don't see myself as a missionary, but at the same time there are a lot of people crying out there that can maybe benefit more by being approached in an indirect way, than being hit over the head with the issue. What the Lord has given me to work with is my music and a specific position in relation to the music business.'

Cockburn sees his faith maturing. He looks back at some of his work and sees it lacking something and he is uncomfortably aware that people might judge him by an immature view which he has since outgrown. Anyone hearing early Cockburn would be conscious of more mystical and spiritual experiential songs while more recently he has emphasised the Christian's response and reaction to what he observes.

His later work is more challenging to the listener on a personal level, reflecting the fact that Cockburn is constantly challenging himself. His 1984 album *Stealing Fire* demonstates on one level his writing skills and another his political-social anger and compassion. Those opposed to the militaristic emphasis in the West will find concurrance. Those who put guns before bread are given no quarter. Equally the album shows that Cockburn is well grounded in Scripture and consequently freed rather than limited by his faith. *Making Contact* and *Sahara Gold* are very sensuous and there is an open celebration of life that can have strong love, strong feelings, strong sensuality. Central America is the subject of the three concluding songs. Cockburn runs a gamut of emotions and because he can utilise words so well he is able to evoke their intensity with considerable effect. He can also write angrily as he does on *If I Had A Rocket Launcher* which emphasises the depth and strength of the Christian's ability to care, and underlines the practical quality of this love. Cockburn has seen real suffering; he has seen for himself squalor, misery, deprivation and sheer waste of precious life. He knows these are things that Christ opposed.

Cockburn's work may not be fashionable and his name may not be widely known but he is bringing important Christian concepts into general rock culture. He makes this important point – 'If you're going to celebrate Christ in your art then the art has got to be of top quality.'

Pot-Pourri

A few years ago it would have been relatively easy to compile a book such as this and to please both artists and fans in doing so. Happily the numbers of Christian pop artists increase all the time. Sadly, one cannot write about all at equal length. If your favourite is only mentioned briefly, forgive me. However, even this pot-pourri is a powerful one comprising people of considerable influence. In one or two instances 'contact' has been lost and they've either moved on, stood still or gone backwards in career and even, though hopefully not, in faith.

Techno Twins

Steve Fairnie and Bev Sage both played with a couple of bands before deciding to team up with Fish & Co., Famous Names and Writz, and now together as The Technos they have emphasised creativity and have a constant thirst for the new and the different that makes some Christians feel uneasy.

Their critics describe them as irreverent, even naughty, but much of the criticism arises from misunderstanding their art and their goals. Bev is a former fashion student who enjoys dressing up and can look startling. Steve spent years contemplating design at the Royal College of Art. When two genuinely innovative people decide to stun, shock, amuse and inform the effect can be electric. Their style is definitely not church hall oriented.

They've toured as support to numerous well-known bands and their genuine professional skills have brought wide acclaim. They've worked at getting a hit single and have almost made it but not quite. *Falling In Love Again* was a real gas of a record, a delightful tongue-in cheek disco pulser that deserved big things but stayed in the lower end of the charts.

In the 1980s they've explored several musical styles and the results of their fascination for 1940s film memorabilia have included *Falling In Love Again* and a version of *In The Mood* rearranged as weird, fantastic modern dance music. They often write their own material, *Nightime Heaven* being one of their most interesting efforts of the eighties.

They've also made a few magazine covers in their time including *Today* (then *Crusade*). Some subscribers must have wondered if they'd got the right magazine!

Their albums include *The Techno Orchestra* and the stunning *Technostalgia*. In 1985 they released *Foreign Land* and presented some of its material at that year's Greenbelt. One big new song in their repertoire has been *Crying In The Rain*, and with a new record contract with Warner Brothers the Technos have bright future ahead of them.

How do they see their future in the second half of the 1980s? 'A Christian couple making a living out of being creative' they reply. They enjoy their lives and they enjoy the church they go to.

Cindy Kent

In the 1960s Britain resounded to the sound of The Settlers. They seemed to fill the airwaves but failed to accumulate vital hit records and had to be content with just one succes, *The Lightning Tree* which reached 36.

The lead singer was a vivacious, attractive girl from the Midlands called Cindy Kent. When her elder sister, who had become a Christian at a holiday camp, took Cindy to a Congregational chapel then, as she says, 'the penny dropped' and it was a case of saying 'I put my name into John 3:16.'

The other two group members Mike Jones and John Fyffe, had met at a Birmingham college in September 1962. They wanted to enter a Modern Groups' Competion in the Isle of Man but needed four people. Mike had met Cindy a few months earlier and asked her to join them and they found Mansel Davies, playing in a folk club. They won the competition, but not without mishap. Cindy fell from one of the island's horse-trams and cracked two ribs. She insisted on singing even though ribs were tightly bound in plaster! She stole the show then and arguably continued to do so. Certainly it was her vibrant faith that took the group onto major religious TV and radio programmes, as well as touring clubs and halls.

Cindy was a long-legged 5ft 5in girl with green-grey eyes and fair hair. She was a former pupil of Barclay Green Grammar School for Girls and for a time had been a secretary. She admired female singers Ella Fitzgerald and

Cleo Laine and her favourite male artist was certainly Cliff Richard.

She was born 7 August, 1945 in West Bromwich, Staffordshire and was christened Cynthia by her parents William and Iris Kent. Her father died when she was sixteen. She had a sister, Anne. Initially she was attracted by tambourine and guitar but soon realised her main talent was her voice.

The group had a string of record releases that promised success. Among their records were *On The Other Side,* part-written by Tom Springfield; *Settle Down;* the Lennon and McCartney song, *Nowhere Man;* Gordon Lightfoot's *Early Morning Rain;* their own composition *Till Winter Follows Spring* and, early in their career, *When It's Gonna Be My Turn.* This was a question they asked themselves as others charted. And there were three they called their 'lost hits'! One was *Don't Let The Rain Come Down.* They rehearsed it and they planned it as their next single but the record company said otherwise. Subsequently, Ronnie Hilton waxed it and it made the top 20.

They thought of recording Dylan's *Tambourine Man* but when they heard Dylan was going to release it they withdrew. However, Dylan did not issue it, but the Byrds did and they had a chart-topper. Then there was *Nowhere Man.* Some people thought they were attempting to jump on a popular bandwagon but others had successfully recorded Beatle songs. Unfortunately the Beatles released their version around the same time.

In addition to recording together they sang carols at St Martin In The Fields, one of London's most famous churches and the group recorded an album *Sing A New Song* in aid of a poverty relief programme. Cindy told the press 'Because I am a practising Christian and against permissiveness, people expect me to be nutty . . . or dull. I hope I'm neither!' She certainly wasn't.

The group toured extensively overseas and at home they played a wide variety of venues. At the Savoy Hotel Cindy had the audience enthusiastically clapping the rhythm of the Hebrew 'Hora' which she led with gusto. They appeared in a special Tyne Tees show from St Nicholas's Cathedral, Newcastle; sang on *We Want To Sing* (BBC TV); appeared at Manchester's famous Golden Garter and had several series for Tyne Tees that were screened nationwide. The girl who collected pictures of Snoopy and ensured the group van was painted in her favourite colours, found herself starring with the rest of the group in a new ATV show *Songs That Matter* which replaced *Stars On Sunday*. She said 'We will be trying very hard to put over the message of Christianity. TV is the medium of the moment. I feel that if Jesus were here today he would appear on TV.'

She attended the same church as Cliff and Cliff, Cindy and the Settlers did concerts together right across Europe. It was a busy group who for all its popularity just couldn't shift records, as the trade would say. Eventually Cindy left and later the very different group, the New Settlers was formed.

Cindy developed a solo career, released some records and began concert and media work, with both continuing in the 1980s. She has also diversified into radio, working for commercial stations and also BBC Radio One.

When she looks back she often wonders how her faith survived. She was the only Christian in The Settlers. 'After long discussions on religion I was exhausted at 3 a.m.!' and she comments 'it is easier to be a Christian when you are with others – the tests come when you are not.' She has a description of her witness which she rather likes, 'I think of Christianity as a block of gold. I wouldn't drop it on anyone, but I like to chip bits off and use them as every day currency.'

These days she has a young child James, as well as various cats and dogs, and she undertakes extensive media work. She is a great example of how a pop singer can find Jesus and never let go. Of course, *He* never lets go.

Tania Maria

Tania Maria belongs to a growing band of artists who specifically mention God or Jesus on their album sleeves. While the idea makes some people feel embarassed and self-conscious, for others it is an obvious means of expression.

Tania has been building a reputation in America for quality vocal work. Her background has given her a good grounding, with classical piano from the age of seven and by twelve she was adept at several styles including dance band music. Until she was seventeen there was no thought of using her voice. 'Up to that point, I'd thought that singing was vulgar but it was so much fun that I soon changed my mind.' She studied law for a while since a singing career seemed too uncertain but at twenty-three she decided to become a professional musician.

The Brazilian lady chose to work the hard way in nightclubs. 'It was like a school you have to go to – you do it because you need the preparation. I knew I wouldn't be there forever.' She was also aware that in Brazil it's very hard to be accepted as a musician if you're a woman, you're supposed to be only a housewife. She says, 'I just wanted to be seen as somebody who makes good music.'

Eventually she moved to Paris. She cut five LP's for European labels then she signed with Manhattan Records and they released *Made In New York*. She stands poised for major fame and sees God as central to her life and living.

Petra

This US pop-rock band have been together a long time – the members met at Bible school in Indiana. Each came from a rock and roll background and believed their future lay in Christian rock music. They knew there were some people that would listen only to rock music and they wanted to communicate the Gospel to those people. They chose the name Petra because it means 'rock', it's the word Jesus used when he said 'Upon this rock I will build my church'. It's upon the testimony of Jesus Christ that the group is built.

After thirteen years recording and touring, a link between A&M and Star Song gave them their first break on the secular scene in 1985. They were signed on the basis of their musical strength and the fact that the band was amongst those US bands drawing the best concert crowds. Their religious company was selling some 500,000 copies of their more recent releases and it was obviously time their music and message was heard by a far larger audience than had been reached largely through religious radio channels.

The basis for their music has always been Scripture. They paid special attention to Psalm 33:3 where the words 'Sing unto Him a new song, play skilfully with a loud noise' can be found. Their melodic, pop-rock featuring smooth harmonies and soaring instrumental passages fit this description well. They've also found an enormous response that has gone far beyond admiration for their music; people have found Jesus through their entire testimony.

Charlene

Charlene was born in Hollywood to Italian parents. She was one of the few white artists signed to Motown Records and Berry Gordy, the company's founder believed she could be a major star. She worked with some Motown producers, including the legendary artist Smokey Robinson, and met Ron Miller who wrote a song for her entitled *I've Never Been To Me,* a deep look into some of the sad and painful moments of her life and seeming inability to find the true self. The song was recorded and, like hundreds of others each and every week, it achieved little though it did make a brief entry into the US top 100. She recorded some more for Motown but when these bore no fruit she quit the music scene, somewhat disillusioned. For a girl who had dropped out of school at 16, become pregnant and married, then later divorced, this further blow was numbing. It was bearable only because she found God, Jesus and a personal faith.

She fell in love again and married an Englishman Geoff Oliver. They made their home in Essex in the UK. For a time she worked with British Youth for Christ and she also found a new record contract with the company Chapel Lane. At this point a development occurred which was to have considerable impact upon her. Unknown to Charlene her single had been re-issued in America and one morning in the early hours she received a call to tell her it was becoming big in the US charts.

It started a lot of other chart movements as people

picked up on the record and it was freshly serviced to DJs and reviewers all over the world. In 1982 it topped the UK charts bringing with its success a host of TV invitations and innumerable interviews. She could hardly believe it – she was very much news. It topped the Australian, Irish and Canadian charts and rested at three in the USA. Her early material was in demand and Motown planned new recordings. The Chapel Lane album would contain the Commodores song *Jesus Is Love* with extra power from the black gospel Majestic Choir. British musicians Dave Cooke and back-up ladies of Nutshell and Network 3, Mo Turner and Annie McCaig lent their playing and vocal skills. In America Cindy and Stevie Wonder recorded the powerful duet *Used To Be* – with its strong religious message.

This sudden but welcome success, however, was spoiled by the many critical remarks over the lyrics of *I've Never Been To Me*. It was certainly frank. She pointed out it was written and sung before she became a Christian. She couldn't add a postscript and say she was now a Christian and had asked for forgiveness. Nor could she talk of how she knew Christ had died for her. It was all rather awkward. Where it was possible she told of her new life and the hit gave her many opportunities for making more music for both general and Christian audiences.

Her music moves in MOR territory, not quite rock. But music, like the Gospel, is free for all.

Amy Grant

It had to come – Amy Grant could not remain a big seller only in the religious record market. In 1985 she soared up the US charts with *Find A Way*, increasing her already enormous appeal. A headline in the journal *Rolling Stone* had announced 'Amy Grant Wants To Put God In The Charts' and she did! In itself it was quite remarkable that such a big magazine had given space to Amy and the Jesus Music scene for the religious music world is generally seen as some kind of backwater. However, although once it was a minority influence, now the Jesus Music world, especially in America, has become an important part of the music scene. Further, as this book shows, many Christian artists are signed with secular record companies.

Amy Grant's appearance on the A&M label was the result of a distribution deal between Word and the former company. A&M President Gil Friesen told his staff that he expected a two million sale for Amy's album *Unguarded*. He took a major ad in the large US trade journal *Billboard* to announce his optimism. But he isn't the only person with a message. Amy has one too. 'I really feel like I've got something to say . . . I've got something really good to say. It makes me want a lot of people to hear it.'

When Amy found herself confronting record company personnel she chose her words carefully. She knew full well that artists come and go and that the record executives have seen it many times. She gave a clever speech insisting that most people would like a world built upon Christian principles – 'cause it means truth and love and kindness and compassion', she declared. 'Everybody wants hope' and she painted the sad picture of teen suicides and craziness. She said 'It's pretty bleak out there, pretty dark.' Then she explained, 'So what we are trying to do is take Christian principles and make them understandable. Even if it doesn't say Jesus, it doesn't matter. For someone whose heart is open – some kid sitting in his room at night, lonely, just thinking, "My world is bleak" – that's the time that we hope this record can say something deeper than "Hey, pull down your pants, I'm going to show you what love really is." '

It had impact.

Her musical ministry has had impact too. She has won Grammy and Dove Awards for her recorded music; her concerts have been sell-outs at some big locations, and one journalist wrote, 'Amy Grant is to Christian pop music what Michael Jackson is to the rest of the recording world'. Her music had possibly altered the perspectives and lives of countless young people.

Her background was a prosperous one. She was the youngest of four daughters of a doctor and his wife. She was born in Augusta, Georgia, and after living for a while in Houston, Texas, the family settled in Nashville, the country recording capital. As a young teenager she did some pretty ordinary jobs such as sweeping floors and de-magnetizing tape heads in a Nashville studio. She made a tape and the right people heard it, by telephone! On the strength of a long distance audition she had a contract and her career began.

She was thrilled to be signed with the religious record company Word. 'I'm a Christian and I want to sing about it.'

Her first secular album release was her ninth all told. It's far more powerful and rocky than some previous ones but the budget was higher and it has been more important in view of the deal between Word and A&M. Amy says, 'I want my music to come across as vulnerable, reachable, hopeful, and having a conscience. I don't want to *be* a conscience, but I want my music to encourage someone to be a whole person.'

She knows that can only be achieved in a living relationship with Jesus born from personal surrender. She made her commitment in the seventh grade at school.

'It was on a Wednesday night, and I just felt that I needed to make a commitment to the Lord and be baptized so I did.' Some conflicts arose from the decision and she would sometimes fight against its implications. She learnt the value of a daily quiet time of worship and prayer; minutes when she could give all her attention to the Lord drawing closer to her. Her smiling, happy, open, honest and friendly self has made a lot of friends and her nature and personality is a great testimony to her faith.

Many people are praying that her wider ministry will see her grow in her own deep-felt beliefs and at the same time win a response from others to the Lord who underlies her music and vocation.

The Alarm

The Alarm made a great deal of noise singing *68 Guns*, their first British chart success. In front was a committed Christian by the name of Mike Peters. The band has some punkish elements but reflects a number of influences including rock, reggae and folk.

Underlying everything has been a frenetic energy level that can leave the listener feeling exhausted. Perhaps the reason for Mike's energy lies in his regular running, up to eight miles each morning. He caught the running bug after meeting a young boy called Alexander who cannot run because he's disabled with cerebral palsy. 'It just made me realise I've got everything and that persuaded me to take up running seriously.' In 1985 he wanted to enter the now famous London Marathon but since it fell in the middle of an Alarm tour he had to give up the idea.

The Alarm began in the Welsh town of Rhyl with the name derived from the very first song they wrote together, *Alarm, Alarm*. Originally they were an acoustic act rather than the bombastic group they were to become. They saved pennies and released a debut single *Unsafe Building* on their own label. By 1982 they had begun attracting attention in the London area and, in addition to building up a core of fans who went everywhere with them, they had begun to attract the notice of the media.

By the summer of 1983 they had their first headline tour of Britain and, with a growing friendship between themselves and U2, they supported the Irish group in their

Stateside gigs. The connection with U2 won them immediate media notice. Mike and Bono came together on stage, when The Alarm were supporting U2, and sang Dylan's *Knockin' On Heaven's Door*. They are both Christians and show the desire to communicate this faith through their music while understanding the pressure their work puts on their Christian growth.

The Alarm's popularity increased and their record company IRS issued a five-track EP of the group's material. It spent 16 weeks on the American *Billboard* chart which was quite remarkable considering the group was not a mainline band in the US. Then came their recording of *68 Guns*. It reached the top 20 in Britain and made the US charts also. An interesting story surrounds the record in America. The Alarm were en-route to Boston when the US Highway Patrol flagged them down. They thought the worst and at very least reckoned they would receive a speeding ticket. To their surprise they were handed a telegram which bore the news that *68 Guns* had charted on its first week of release and so was safely in the all-important *Billboard* Hot 100. They had a good laugh and accepted with delight the patrol officer's wish – 'have a good day!'.

That was the start of a career that has given them a few hits and had its ups and downs, but which is still going strong in the mid-1980s both in Britain and America. They had a major British hit single in 1986 entitled *Spirit of '76*. Crowds have loved numbers such as *The Stand, Blaze Of Glory, As The Dawn Comes Breaking Through* and *One Step Closer To Home* and the group is one of Britain's best loved live acts. Their rendition of *This Train Is Bound For Glory* might be unexpected for some of the audience but not those aware of Mike's Christian commitment. He's the only professed Christian in the group and the band is a straightforward rock'n'roll outfit with designs on taking the rock world apart. Mike says he hopes their lyrics challenge people not to take everything at face value. 'The answer has to be found by the person' and he adds 'We have a faith but the beliefs? – they're personal.'

He reads the Bible a lot and prays regularly. He sees a war going on out there in the world and 'the Lord is looking for people for an army, not with machine guns. In that army there are different divisions. I think the Lord wants a secret service where people don't know who the agents are.'

He says The Alarm is not a political band. 'Only personal politics – the individual.' For him it comes down to understanding Jesus and he claims the right to express his understanding in the music he plays best even though this is not to everyone's taste. As *Strait* writer Graham Langley said, 'Remember labels breed prejudice. Don't tag them "Christian" (The Alarm) and pursue them for the sake of it. Label them "The Alarm" enjoy them and let their punk following enjoy them too. If you don't like punk, wouldn't dream of going to a Clash gig and dislike loud rebellious noise, then don't go and see them. Stay at home with a cup of hot cocoa and your Simon and Garfunkel video.'

Enough said!

DeBarge

America's teen sensation DeBarge have been constantly compared with The Jacksons and The Ritchie Family by music journalists looking for quick copy. The comparison may be valid to a limited extent but only DeBarge released the smash hit single *Rhythm Of The Night*. This was the title track of an album which itself sold several million worldwide and established the group as the best thing Motown has.

In the US success had come earlier and other smash hits have included *I Like It, All This Love, Time Will Reveal* and *In A Special Way*.

Their readiness to say they are Christians and to attribute their success to Jesus has been a consistent feature of interviews with them. They may not please some people with the kind of songs they sing nor with their presentation but no one can fault their public declaration of faith. It is bold and it can be costly. DeBarge know that but they keep on giving their testimony.

Their roots go back to a gospel upbringing and Ma DeBarge's insistence they travel on the right road and not get lost in the nasty bushes that tend to grow on the side!

Mark DeBarge says, 'We believe in God and we have a faith that will see us through. We praise Him for the good and the bad. I think we know better from having been through temptation, but sometimes the temptation is very strong!' He adds, 'the glory is to God.'

Lone Justice

Music writers and critics have been forecasting great things for the American band Lone Justice. There has been some criticism but, overall, the music press has expressed appreciation of their music. The group has also been attracting fans from the world of rock and country. Bob Dylan likes them, so does Dolly Parton and Tom Petty.

Maria McKey is the vivacious attractive girl who fronts the band. Rock and roll lacks glamour for her and she emphasised to the press that she is not like Madona; she doesn't want comparisons thank you. Maria is also the band's songwriter but most people hear her voice before they read the small print of the credits.

The group enjoy music from people like U2 and X, and, for diversity, Los Lobos. To play themselves they choose a mix of psychedelic and country. The psychedelic note isn't too surprising for apart from its return to popularity in the mid-1980s Maria's brother Bryan was a member of the memorable Love who recorded one of the great albums of all time – *Forever Changes* on Elektra.

Their music isn't totally original but their energy and enthusiasm puts them ahead of many others. The vocals on their debut album *Lone Justice,* are punched out with authority and brashness and the guitar work is raunchy even if some of the riffs sound a little familiar at times. The album's first song is *East Of Eden* and if Maria hasn't commented on the Fall she has directly told of her Christian faith. Her strong faith in God comes out in her song writing and this has been observed by rock writers for the secular press. No criticism has been levelled, the music is too powerful. Maria happily tells of her church-going and she expresses how her faith is a unifying factor in her life. *You Are The Light* is something special on their album.

The group began in 1982 but it was not until 1985 they began to be widely heard and noticed, and they could certainly be one of the big outfits of the rest of this decade. It's great knowing that such a fine artist as Maria is a Christian.

And they play such good music!

Teri De Sario

1980 saw Teri De Sario join forces with H.W. Casey of K.C. and the Sunshine Band for a major top 40 hit *Yes, I'm Ready*. In America she found further acclaim with two singles from her first album of solely Christian material – *A Call To Us All* spawned *I Dedicate All My Love To You* and *Battleline*. Americans also know her as the voice behind a Sony television commercial that produced the number one hit *Overnight Success*.

She is described as a 'woman with explosive power,' and possessed with a voice that is 'bright and compassionate.' Her song lyrics are polished, poetic and profound, and they form a good partnership with the upbeat melodies and rhythms composed by her husband-producer Bill Purse.

Teri's early life followed a not unfamiliar pattern. For a while she had a strong faith but during her teens she pushed aside her religious experience. She was born to Italian Catholic parents but the family fell out with the church and she was baptized Lutheran. She regarded this early experience as irrelevant and viewed religion as 'archaic and hypocritical.' Her first marriage at the age of 20 proved disastrous. When the second was faring badly she re-sought and discovered a new vibrant religious experience. She began to write songs that talked of her new faith.

She signed a contract with Word Records and was described as someone who was a 'non-denominational

Protestant'. Later she and some friends began to look at modern catholicism. This time she was attracted and eventually became a convert.

She talks of Christianity this way: 'As Christians we must dig for our faith, take the teachings of Christ seriously, and then as peacemakers and friends to all, work to build a more dynamic community where love may be fully realised.' Certainly many see her songs overflowing with love and faith-filled conviction. She may not see all the obstacles that have divided much of christendom into Catholic and Protestant but she is insistent that there is much common ground between both and says, 'It is crucial for us to learn to live out our lives in unity with Jesus Christ lest we remain a terrible scandal to the non-Christian world.'

All this sounds a far cry from the girl who experienced chart fame but Teri De Sario doesn't see why people should create even more divisions! She sings because the Lord has given her a voice and music. And she is grateful.

Violent Femmes
(Gordon Gano)

'Indie' bands find radio airplay scarce. They depend largely on fanzine music press coverage and just sometimes they find a real fan amongst the more popular and widely sold music papers. Life hasn't been easy for American group Violent Femmes. They have a cult following and just enough in their music and make-up to attract the interest of a major record company in Britain. Their 1986 album *The Blind Leading The Blind* did not have the brilliance of *Hallowed Ground* with the greater number of good tracks. The more recent however caught the ear in cuts *No Killing, Cold Canyon* and *Faith*.

Features Editor of *Strait,* Martin Wroe describes their music as 'a salacious musical adventure in stark, primitive bare-boned country-punk-gospel-blues-jazz-swing-rude-rock-and-roll'. It is a double-bass, a set of stand-up drums, some very unclean horns, a snarling guitar and Gordon Gano's wailing and gnashing of teeth laid down on top.

Gano is the Christian in the band. British music weekly *Melody Maker* termed him 'a card-carrying Baptist' and he is a member of Mount Moriah Baptist Church in Milwaukee. He says, 'The two things I dislike about touring are not being able to be with loved ones and not being able to go to church. Sometimes if I'm in New York where I know a church, I can just roll out of bed, throw on some clothes, stumble out of the door and wake up in that church.'

Gano's dad is both a minister and a professional actor! Minister's sons (or daughters) seem to either follow the faith avidly or rebel. Sometimes they rebel against the unrealistic expectations that people have of ministers' kids and the pressures to behave or dress in certain ways. It can be hard in the peer group also. Gordon became a rebel although at first he did seek a church where there was excitement, and in his travels he found a black church. 'It was wilder and freer than my upbringing. I enjoyed the style of music a lot more but it wasn't just artistic or aesthetic reasons that I was going for . . . I enjoyed the style of preaching too. It really excited me.'

Gano believes the group's songs make people think and in keeping with more thoughtful 'indie' bands The Violent Femmes have attracted considerable personal commitment from followers. But he admits freely that the subject matter of their music shocks some people. There is no division of life into sacred and secular and Gano talks about Jesus freely without adopting a religious hat for the occasion or seeking the 'right' setting.

He has another band which even ten years on from the British music explosion of 1976 can still be called a punk outfit but more precisely a 'punk-gospel' outfit. He calls the band The Mercy Seat. The personnel is two guys and two girls and they sing material made famous in the 1950s by people like James Cleveland and the Davis Sisters. Here, the Christian message is more explicit and direct. The band was among the early bookings for the Greenbelt Festival '86.

I met Gano during 1986 when the band was promoting *The Blind Leading The Blind* and a single, *Children Of The Revolution*.

The single song was originally a hit for T. Rex in 1972, after the late Sixties flower power revolution. When I questioned Gano on his odd choice of reviving what seemed a 'period-piece' he told me that though times have changed there is still a hunger for truth and, more so, for personal identity. Gano's music may not attract everyone and that doesn't worry him; his concern is that people should at very least explore the point, purpose and meaning of Jesus's life.

And more . . .

It's difficult to end this book for the wonderful reason that rock artists continue to give their lives to Christ. I could have written about Sal Solo, ex-Classix Nouveau, friend of Nick Beggs and a British chart entrant with material that reflects his faith. Or long-time star hit-maker Alvin Stardust, and Paul Jones, ex-Manfred Man and Blues Band.

So too there is Julie Hadwen, lead singer with a two-hit British group Big Sound Authority. She went forward to make her commitment at the Penze Christian Fellowship one night during 1985. *This House* and *A Bad Town* were their two MCA successes during the first half of 1985.

I could write about the several British Gospel groups who have charted in the 1980s and, more so, I could predict that Steve Taylor will find a wide, wide market with his perceptive and stimulating lyrics and music. Taylor's pop musical comedy *Nothing To Lose,* albums *I Want To Be A Clone* and *Meltdown* are superior to much current rock. Taylor has the right kind of personality as well. And it will be no surprise if Barnabas or the Resurrection Band find success. Then there are rock people like Roger McGuinn, Joe English, Bonnie Bramlett, Mylon Le Fevre . . . country people like George Hamilton IVth and Glen Campbell . . . the list goes on and on and will grow.

And grow!!!!!

PRESENTING
TONY CAMPOLO ON VIDEO

IT'S FRIDAY, BUT SUNDAY'S COMIN'

"I'm not ashamed of the Gospel of Christ, because the Gospel of Christ meets every need of every human being on this planet."

IT'S FRIDAY, BUT SUNDAY'S COMIN' is a powerful message that has motivated Christian congregations around the country to seek a deeper, more costly commitment to Christ.

Dr Campolo's sharp, honest humour makes us laugh at our own short sightedness. His down to earth insight and persuasive arguments compel us to responsible action.

IT'S FRIDAY, BUT SUNDAY'S COMIN' video is just one of over 20 videos currently available.

For further details of Word videos and other Word products please complete the coupon below.

Please send me information on:

Word Records/Cassettes	☐	Books	☐
Lifelifter Cassettes	☐	Video	☐

(Please tick items of interest)

Name...

Address ....

....

Word Publishing
Word (UK) Ltd
9 Holdom Avenue, Bletchley,
Milton Keynes, MK1 1QU